Time Being

Jimmy

w/
Lots
O
Love —

Jim

ALSO BY JOSEPH TORRA

FICTION

Gas Station
Tony Luongo
My Ground
The Bystander's Scrapbook
They Say
What's So Funny

POETRY

16 Paintings
Domino Sessions
Keep Watching the Sky
August Letter to My Wife and Daughters
After the Chinese
Watteau Sky (with Ed Barrett)

Time Being

Joseph Torra

Quale Press

On the front cover: a digitally altered photograph
by Molly Torra

The author thanks the editors of *Polis* and *Eoagh: A Journal of
the Arts*, where sections of *Time Being* previously appeared.

ISBN: 978–1–935835-06-6 trade paperback edition

LCCN: 2012934393

Quale Press
www.quale.com

Time Being

An improvisation
December 2006 – December 2007

For Molly, Julia and Celeste

AT ONE POINT IN HIS LIFE LIEH-TZU DECIDED THAT ALL HIS learning was shallow so he settled into domestic life cooked for his wife did the housework tended to the pigs trying to be kind and for three years never left home until finally he was no longer a carved piece of jade but an unhewn block of wood guy in the café says you teachers have it made all them vacations too I try to explain I'm only an adjunct but he interrupts and all them good benefits doctor's appointment cholesterol one level's high one low good category bad category I don't know if I should work as a substitute teacher on my semester break pull the plastic trash bag out of the plastic trash can pistachio shells all over the kitchen floor sweep the

shells curse under my breath Celeste wants to wear
the same pink socks she's worn the last two days put
on clean ones but I like these Daddy and on the way
to school math story problem how many pizzas we
ordered how many total slices how many are left she
says Daddy leave me alone Maureen's strong meaty
arms smiles works my bad shoulder press this way
push that way do this one at home with your hand
around your back hooks me to a machine sends
electric current through wires to my shoulder
shocks the nerve-points for fifteen minutes on the
way out an older Haitian woman yells at her thera-
pist through a translator that her therapist is making
her leg worse she's not coming back why call them
sonnets if they don't follow the traditional sonnet
form Celeste and Julia eat bacon pizza juice and
vitamins for breakfast Williams' "January" think of it
as a movie with various cuts write one yourself at
work in my office paintings posters broadsides on
the wall twenty-three poems in the spirit of WCW's
"January" the way you make your jumps sharp line
breaks lively rhythms don't need to say it that's
obvious here's where you're really making it happen
Corbett's Copley Square poems Kaufman's God you
are just an empty refrigerator with a dead child
inside incognito in the debris of the modern junk-
pile Bill calls Bev's Christmas bread and cookies
ready Molly strings the lights the girls divide the

decorations bargaining until the bulbs split between them Molly says she's gone all out for the girls means don't ask how much old student phones finally paid money he owed can I write a letter stating that he took my class and did his work Dear Professor Torra could you write me a letter of recommendation for a cash award grant Hispanic cashier at Target asks is their mother Asian Julia says no we're adopted several awkward moments she rings up our candy canes winter socks oh they're so cute I can see why you adopted them more silence are they sisters yes I respond yes they are sisters she hands me my receipt and bag they're so cute have a nice day bottom of Winter Hill Broadway illegals congregate carry beer coolers for lunch buckets eye out for truck or van driven some contractor looking to pick up painters laborers carpenters brick layers maybe a day or two maybe a week there's more men than work last day of class Li Po Tu Fu Mei Yao Chen Li Ching Chao like hip hoppers and rappers one student says the way they correspond with each other four loads of laundry Celeste changes three times a day my socks underwear five and six towels at a time sheets pillowcases hang rock and roll t-shirts in the basement Iggy Lou Patti Ramones Richard Hell Radio Birdman Johnny Thunders strung up on the line to dry snot so far from punk to laundry the girls put three dozen candy canes on the tree they've eaten five how many are left good math problem for Celeste but I only ate two and Julia ate three doesn't matter I just want to know how many are left on the tree play my acoustic Julia and Celeste sing "Mad World" Celeste has homework on weekends plus special projects at the end of the semester students turn in a portfolio if they come to class do the reading and writing they get an A my neighbor killed three deer with his bow and arrow he sat in a tree until a deer came close enough sometimes the deer don't die right away because the arrow not so deadly as bullet the wounded deer eventually bed down and bleed out he gives me venison sausage and a piece of tenderloin the tenderloin comes from a big old buck gamey and tough marinate in wine for a day there's still mushrooms I picked in the fall cook the venison with wild mushrooms good year for mushrooms all of the rain hen-of-the-woods in abundance lots of painted boletes under the white pines along the Winchester Reservoir light today on Broadway's a flat beige washes old red-bricks and white aluminum-sided three-deckers down Broadway clear to Charlestown Portuguese neighbor died young then his widow wore black then she sold the place new folks filled in the fishpond and took out the fountain my neighbor had taken so much pleasure in skill saws nail guns pound guys talk loud upstairs Julia naps Celeste plays with her dolls and

doll house Sparky drools on the sofa next to Julia
Celeste's wind-up clock on my studio wall Celeste's
name on the face of the clock tick-tock two-twenty-
two and how many seconds cunt is more difficult to
write than cock someone says I take pleasure in dis-
pute it's not about pleasure I have no choice and
can't do otherwise I'm afraid the girls watch too
much television Julia eats corn bread toast and
bacon Celeste taquitos finish your juice take your
vitamins it's thirty years I've been wiping asses on
weekends and I'm tired of it Molly says off to hospi-
tal shift Sunday morning six-thirty dark and cold out
there percentage of men shrinking in the state work
force local news is always one nerdy white newsman
and one sexy white blonde newswoman weather
people go either way maybe nerdy white guy bald
okay or ethnic women sports is where a black man
can most easily can make a stand vacuum living
room sweep kitchen floor call Big Brother take the
kids' old bedroom dressers from front porch Chinese
soup wings dumplings bean curd with black mush-
rooms noodles sesame beef and pan fried fish I'm
gonna eat til I drop Julia says looking down Broad-
way Winter Hill Bunker Hill Monument like a sharp
Egyptian prick where on a school field trip I grew
dizzy climbing the spiral staircase and the smell of
piss live when it is time to live die when it is time to
die it's easy for Lieh-tzu to say Celeste what do you

want to write in your weekend journal how about
ballet and taking care of Sparky storm windows in
warmer now they don't call me into sub until the last
minute just when I think I will have a day free the
phone rings hello Joe it's Mary can you work today
newsman is a correct word while newswoman pops
up typo floor needs mopping but I'll put it off Celeste
calls from upstairs Dad do you want me no but come
down here give me a kiss feet thump down the base-
ment stairs onto my lap kiss ooh that's fast these
words I type Dad are you glad that I gave you my
clock so you'll know what time it is right now it is
nine-fifteen Dad can I have an apple four in the
morning fears and failure the hammering sounds
like drumming from places far away big shaggy
saggy old white pines practice Chi Kung in the
breeze dwarfing the small brown wooden house
Mike calls leaves a message call me bye I call Frank
leave a message Frank calls back hangs up on me
because of what I say about his wife can you use a
phrase like win men's hearts anymore maybe words
are abnormal maybe middle of the night obsessions
can get a word in edgewise the young man in the
package store wants a keg and seems so proud must
be his first call my mother how's the girls good Ma
how's the girls good Ma so how are the girls doing
Dad can I read something to you yes Julia it's about
Inca Gods there were many but I chose two I'm sup-

posed to write one paragraph is that one paragraph
that's at least two Molly phones from work how's it
going brutal but time's flying I can't imagine a job
where you wipe some old psycho's ass while he
swears and swings his fists at you and that's the best
part of your day Derek reads from his odes to Katie
Couric his Katie his Couric Jen Olin reads odes to
medications her Depakote with a Lamictal chaser
gray day driving over the Zakim Bridge traffic's light
going into the tunnel give the bottle of wine to Peter
I hope that you drink of course I drink so long it's
been a good semester good luck drop in my office
and say hello any time Celeste's homework list ten
rights animals should have and use at least five of
this week's spelling words in your list finish your
apple pick a book we'll read there's give and pull to
things the electrician says ordering another espresso
if you sleep for ninety-nine out of one hundred days
your sense of what is dream and what is waking
reality will adjust accordingly my office at school is
cold I cannot get the air conditioner to turn off sit
with winter coat draped over my shoulders you
don't have any books in your office never know
when I'll have to pack up and move the black man
who works the grill calls all the men brother calls
the women hon I order a chicken quesadilla hold the
sour cream how long do you want me to hold it for
brother I wish I could respond to things without

considering consequences the hammer and the skill saw pills in plastic bottles Sparky barks something inside the wall the deer I shoot looks like Sparky its intestines spill from the wound but he still breathes my cousin Tony's father dies and I hold the deer under water in a barrel to put it out of its misery I wake to the sound of bubbles Maureen caught a cold from her son and there's a lot of whooping cough going around his school hooks me up to the machine see you in a few minutes and in the curtained section next door how's the neck I think it's a little better this week it wasn't aching they're both going to Florida she has family I thought you were a snow boarder I am but my girlfriend loves manatees we're going to a river and swim with manatees that sounds like great she says she prefaces everything she says with like across the room I spy an elderly man with a pot belly in a black and white striped mime shirt lifting his bare pale weighted leg up and down oh Maureen you're so rough setting herself upon me put your elbow on my arm press your hand against mine push down upon my shoulder with all her might power-stretching my arm straight out it might pop the socket how far is Busch Gardens from Tampa I don't know off-hand but my sister would I can see sixteen houses from our house front back side angles I'd love to have the yard where the fishpond used to be big enough for a good vegetable garden he gave me cucumbers and tomatoes until I asked if his kid might not play the drums so late during the week he stopped talking to me never another hello a few years pass I see his wife wearing black then she sells the house at my uncle's funeral everyone from my past looks so much older in church my mother wants me to kneel and sit and stand and kneel and sit and kneel and sing and stand but I don't in my cousin Tony's game room dead cinnamon-colored black bear stuffed in mid-step did you kill that where did you kill that my mother's second cousin wants to know dead ducks and geese deer heads and caribou antlers full mount of coyote next to the bear oversize pickerel and bass even a mounted turkey don't be a stranger my newly widowed aunt says don't wait until I die to come around again my cousin Marie says I gave her her first cigarette good eggplant sausages are delicious did you try some salad I only believe in heaven and earth metaphorically one whole chicken celery carrots onions herbs salt and pepper boil in big pot remove juicy meat from bones strain the broth toss in chicken pieces and tri-colored wagon wheel pasta I'm trapped inside an old wooden tenement house can't find my way out walking corridors up and down stairs I come upon an aging black man in the hall points to a door that leads to an alley once outside realize that I don't have any pants on three girls on the sidewalk you don't have pants on I bum a cigarette one of them pulls out a pack and the cigarettes are half the usual length pasta with gorgonzola and pears recipe for Celeste's teacher one recipe from each family to show our diversity Julia eats three bowls of soup at dinner another bowl for breakfast says I could eat this stuff forever don't you kick me the nurse practitioner barks angrily at Julia I'm trying to hold her down arms wrapped around her the nurse practitioner jabs that flu shot hard Julia full-panic hyper-ventilating morning stretches salutations and side twists Molly's Christmas bread two cups of coffee Nick's Christmas card Peace Love Joy Nick in blue overalls knee-high yellow rubber boots arm around a sick cow this time of year morning's dark dreary gray late afternoon low-lying sun glare on windshield blinds why Helen Vendler doesn't review books by poets under the age of fifty presents to wrap drinks with Bill and Ed at Grafton Street run to the package store wine tequila Molly's margaritas scotch Celeste cries because I yelled so I apologize Celeste don't cry think of how much fun we're going to have on Christmas Eve Askold's novel Alice Notley's poems *The Book of Lieh-tzu* if I write a hundred more words I get to have lunch the furnace ignites in the next room the filter needs changing shut the thing down remove metal face plate remove dirty filter replace with clean one struggle to get

metal face plate on correctly or the furnace won't
work wild wacky weather worldwide channel four
blonde and geek say hello in Japanese there'll be a
new pitcher at Yenway Park this year Trust Toad and
his friends ready to recycle Hop To It he's yelling in
Italian bi-polar cancer riddled patient Molly's taking
care of there's no way I'll be out of here on time
today he steps into the café wearing a worn olive
colored Florentine suit and dirty brown shoes long
gray hair bushy wax-tipped mustache noble nose
though in the end a homely man with Italian accent
samples in hand nobody around here carries these
cordials and all the great restaurants in Europe serve
them nurses they got it made the guy in the café
says they make more than the teachers but the
hours aren't so good but both those things are good
jobs for a girl I don't want to forget myself while I
am awake and I want to dream when asleep I'm pay-
ing five hundred a month just for insurance so ben-
efits count don't talk to me about teachers just a
quick reminder about our family breakfast this Fri-
day from 8:00 until 8:45 Molly finishes her baking
Russian tea cookies bourbon balls clean the front
patio pull up the dead weeds pick up litter roll the
garden hose store it away no I won't withstand the
weight of the sky it could cause aching in the shoul-
ders and arms warm this month more early April
than end of December smell wet pine outside I have

worldly ambitions soaking in a warm bath drain
cooled water refill with hot no one else in the house
the workmen speak Spanish boards slam nails jam
ladders bounce sanders sand grinders grind genera-
tors hum fall asleep remember this thought sure I
will remember concentrate on it until I fall asleep
now awake I don't remember sun swings slow low
across the sky painted boletes bright red caps yellow
flesh veil over spores likes soil around white pines
break some pieces onto my pizza the parking lot's
empty wind chops the harbor geese wing this way
and that the Blue Hills hide in mist secretary sneaks
in half hour late nice to see you all set for the holi-
days just about did you try the blueberry scones
someone brought delicious chocolates Celeste reads
me poems sits on my lap eats grapes chocolate chip
cookie and a piece of cranberry bread there's organic
soy milk for the coffee if anyone wants it William
pushes David who slips and falls the teacher takes
William aside then his parents corner him fingers
waving in his face you can't do things like that the
insurance agency phones they need proof that I
turned in my plates I recently sold the old eighty-
three Chevy tractor trailers barreling down the
Expressway edging over lanes guy behind me
flashes his lights and beeps his horn wants me to go
faster or get out of the passing lane but I'm afraid to
pass the tractor trailer there's another one in front

of it means I must pass two so I slow down enough to pull into the right lane guy who was behind me passes on the left honks at me for good measure even in my own heart there are some things that I don't always hi I'm a patient of Doctor Lepore and I wonder if he could see me I once heard that a dentist gassed someone to death morning glow of Christmas tree lights in living room my shadow in mirror yoga stretches as Sparky circles claws on hardwood floor pink tinted eastern sky Sunday morning silent no I will not be seeking re-election as the PTA corresponding secretary nor will I recite the Pledge of Allegiance and I dislike officiating and coffee brewed in big electric pots wait until the light turns green they have to say it in English Spanish Portuguese and Creole how much money we started with how much on the book sale how much on bingo and how much field trips with the price of gas and bus rentals don't forget holiday raffle baskets Julia plays Beethoven on the recorder I'm not sure which things benefit me and which harm me I'm certain there's a person who makes fun of me if my past defines my future I can change my future by re-defining my past but I can't go back and change aspects of my undesirable behavior the will to creation is absolute as I come upon a river too rushing and high to ford I scale the wind and cross the water later I saw Julia and Celeste stranded on an island mid-stream what an unsightly spot on a canvas old Chinese proverb says if you don't know what is far away then look for it nearby empty scales hang even how does someone hot-tempered and vulgar as I find the way Maureen asks what is the significance of the coin strung around my neck the round part responds to the outside and the square governs the inside hmmmm she says how's the arm doing are you working it at home approaching the Winter Solstice if I am changing how do I know I am really changing Julia wants leftover ravioli for breakfast lots of sauce Celeste's footsteps down the stairs can I come in Dad you writing how come you put my name in there what is right vs. what will pay how can one not be disgusted at the vile state I am afraid of the passing seasons it's snowing in San Diego Dear Ms. Gaynor Celeste will not be doing the homework assignment during vacation because it is vacation according to Maureen's measurements my arm is improved there's less chronic discomfort but it still hurts Dear Joe I want to thank you for such a great class I have a new story that I want to submit to The Watermark and I wonder if you would read it and offer feedback before I do Dear Jonathan these next couple of weeks I will be busy with the holidays and my daughters' vacation and semester break if you are not in a rush Dear Substitute thank you for coming in today our schedule is very busy and I'm sure you'll have a wonderful day with these students they are active learners and love to be helpful to you I'm not sitting in my chair William says Gabe farted in it no I didn't says Gabe yes sir yes sir volume is height times length times width symmetric intersecting line perpendicular line rectangle prism cone plane figure edge obtuse angle cylinder if I have to talk to you one more time you go out in the hall I read them a story about kids who save birds on some island near Iceland use highlighters what do you think is an important part of the paragraph no teacher salads on Monday all we got left is chicken nuggets Dear Everyone imagine if everyone thinks abnormal is normal garlic and rosemary roast pork summer squash broccoli baked potatoes Dad when you die am I going to be a teenager or grown up no white Christmas this year one day to the solstice First Alert Doppler says temperatures ranging in the forties maybe chance of rain Julia learning Ocean Form in Kung Fu graceful yet powerful movements Christmas grocery list steak chicken wings good cheeses for the baked pasta sauce makings fresh broccoli oh to see things after the fact like dead ends that change patterns what's the difference between one extra spot who are you subbing for today did you get some pastry there's a lot of stuff back there and coffee and eggnog sick old lady next door the ambulance takes her away never hello from her all the years we've been neighbors only cold stares lots of neighbors in this cramped neighborhood body in world world in body physical therapy tomorrow then visit to the surgeon next day dentist Maureen says sign up for another two weeks of physical therapy surgeon appointment wait forty minutes a woman calls my name hi I'm and I'm a nurse asks me the same questions I've been answering for six months how is the arm right now what kind of pain on a level of one to ten how did it happen how long ago well someone will be in to see you in a second ten minutes later a woman walks in introduces herself physician's assistant I think she's wearing braces begins same questions how did it happen what kind of pain how would you rate it on a scale of one to ten stand up please put your hands inside mine and push place your arms straight up high as they will go try to slide your hand up behind your back she explains that things are unfreezing with physical therapy and in time my arm should be back near a hundred percent and she needs to consult with the doctor and he'll be here to talk with me ten minutes pass the doctor appears shakes my hand hop on the bed how high can you put your hand up and back and out and yes his prognosis is the same as the physician's assistant's of course we'll want to see you again in two months shakes my hand disappears leftover chicken and pork roast cut meat into chunks make a ragu for Winter Solstice supper serve over rigatoni wash going load drying clean kitchen living room and bathroom final grocery run don't forget good napkins Bob says he feels like a ghost walking the streets and neighborhoods everything's changed there are no longer any real neighborhoods in the Boston area buildings are gone so little to recognize he won't pay his bills online because there's too much confusion and potential for problems Julia naps Celeste takes a bubble bath suburbs aglow driving home from Nick and Shira's Christmas Eve party Celeste's eyes on the sky fighting sleep Dad is Santa really true what do you think Celeste well if he's true I don't know how he can get down our chimney maybe he comes in the skylight says Julia we hear "Domenic the Donkey" on the car radio and sing along the new neighbors dig up the back yard lawn why would they do that Molly wants to know maybe a patio they're cooking fish in a big pot over a wood fire sitting around in lawn chairs winter coats and drinking beer Spanish listening to Spanish music Molly asks why would you cook outside in the middle of winter when there's an indoor kitchen ten feet away the artist's statement speaks of perception social commentary pre-conceived notions of reality seeing things that we encounter every day in a different light brown paper bag on a shelf a piece of white picket fence barbed wire rolled around the top a number two yellow pencil sticks out from a white board the clothesline strung across the ceiling clipped with clothespins eight white envelopes inside a glass frame a framed notebook opened to two blank lined sheets of paper Molly sings our old standards while I strum the guitar and sing backup finish with "Silent Night" Christmas night they're in the yard again bundled up on lawn furniture drinking beer listening to music talking Spanish we need a bunch of batteries one of Celeste's new toys takes nine sometimes thoughts that seemed so daunting at four in the morning are meaningless now there will never be an end houses needing new roofs additions siding paint jobs porches windows chimney's rebuilt every year we get one more year out of our front porch Sparky barks at squirrels not cold enough to send them into deeper cover can it be worth worrying about what happens after you die sitting here study chair girls upstairs master of my there outside Davis Square Brooks Pharmacy Doug Holder gives me a copy of Poesy special Outlaw Poetry issue with manifesto and interview with an Outlaw Poet Outlaw Poetry cannot be written by someone teaching in the cushy academy Outlaw Poetry is written by dishwashers and cab drivers people in jail people ready to challenge the world they don't win grants or prizes or publish on university presses Outlaw Poetry can be written in small case letters they'll be as big as Language Poetry even The New Formalists will have a laugh over a Yaddo cocktail darkness rinses the last light from the street lit plastic Santa guards a front porch Julia and I walk Sparky the quiet unsettling until two kids rolling down the sidewalk brand new scooters Sparky growls and barks Julia holds him tight on the leash the countdown to New Years Eve be there for the festivities as we come to you live from First Night o Lord of Loads of Towels please straighten the living room vacuum and bring out the trash Julia and Celeste eat the Christmas baked pasta every meal until gone no make a list for our BJ's run what do we need everything Molly says I can be selfish and need to be eating less since Thanksgiving instead I'm eating more stack of Chinese books on my desk unread *The Chinese Renaissance Old Tales Retold The Importance of Living Wild Grass* hockey sticks crack shouts from the schoolyard kids street hockey thuds from Julia and Celeste's running feet on the floor upstairs blonde anchor says that the government does not require cloned meat to be labeled because cloned meat is safe weather turning chilly but will it snow on First Night Gerald Ford and James Brown dead the painting is finished first one since summer "World in Body Body in World" do you make these titles up or get them from books mix five cups of water with fertilizer spread that an inch thick over the mushroom compost leave in box down the basement we'll be picking our own mushrooms in weeks Dad Dad I'm going to play Game Boy until it drowses me then take a nap soon as I wake up I'll have a snack roll the heavy flat cart aisle to aisle cereal olive oil coffee paper towels soda dish washer soap body soap shampoo milk cream frozen broccoli juice Italian pasta canned tomatoes frozen pizza taquitos macaroni and cheese girls and I unload the car in through the kitchen door like people in Westerns unloading supplies we put it all away can we have a snack now Dad Julia naps a dog barks three hammer strikes truck starts it's more like a yelp the dog more jet roar on the Logan pattern three more strikes sometimes it's almost predictable I don't make paintings to sell but I give them away although the longer I have them the closer we are I don't want to give any of them away I will rise from here to fold the load in the dryer refill it with wet from the washer walk the dog decide what to cook for supper read with Celeste three strikes of the hammer boom boom boom Arthur Killer Kane is Buddha I think that the dog turds belong to the daughter of the dying lady next door I catch her in the act she says she forgot her bag and comes back to pick it up but there's more than one leaving them out there I can tell by the differences between the turds New Year's Eve they hang a man people dance in the streets we

count down from ten until the ball stops then kiss
and hug third grade girl smells like piss same thing
last time I subbed this class Roberto says Jesus didn't
take his medicine today Jesus won't stay in his seat
wanders the room makes throaty noises I need help
I need help too they line up at the desk Cameron
wears a perpetual face of existential despair laughs
loudly at inappropriate times read a book about the
winter that it didn't snow until April 1 Cameron
don't you want to draw no I'm writing a movie script
what is it called it's called it's called I don't remember
what it's called but it's coming out January the ninth
or maybe June second well what is it about it's about
it's about two girls and they have this dream it's
about it's about these characters three boys no five
boys and they travel and they travel to I'll show you
he walks over to the map of the U.S.A. points his
index finger swings it way out over the Atlantic then
back over America out to California down to Texas
over to Florida up the Atlantic coast then he stops
and drops his finger spot on and they go to Virginia
then they find then they find this place they find
this place they go to a hotel a hotel and there's
another movie coming out too after this one Roberto
writes a song on the board performs it what do you
think of the song that's not really his song yes it is
yes it is muscle is very tight today have you been
doing your therapy at home time do your worst

Maureen take down the tree and outside lights pack the stockings and decorations away for another year they meant so much a few weeks ago but I feel hopeless and empty leave the tree on the sidewalk where public works folks pick up now's the countdown to Chinese New Year The Year of the Pig Celeste loves the song "Mad World" sings all day have you heard the latest rumor word has it that Mr. Lyons is on his way to be the next assistant superintendent of schools I'm begging for a transfer out of here I've had it I can't yell at students he says that's not allowed I yell at the students all the time yeah but you're a substitute they're lucky to have you weekend weather-woman pregnant again First Alert Doppler more record-setting highs they didn't fill the prescription I dropped off yesterday after I've been standing in line for forty-five minutes twenty minutes more to fill it Julia takes the ice cream out of my red plastic carry basket I'm going to go exchange this for one that's not melted soon I must face the bottom of the basement stairs boxes containing things unknown plus old computers fishing gear broken electric pasta maker broken acoustic guitar window screens kitchen supplies tools books a microwave oven that doesn't work kids' toys usable gardening stuff busted reading lamp empty oxygen tanks from filling party balloons leftover Christmas supplies that haven't made it up to the attic an automobile tire the kitchen floor needs a wet mop several loads of laundry Celeste ballet at eleven Julia and I drop her off and do today's errands will I come into the school and talk with eighth graders about writing short stories character and plot Tuesday and Thursday next week ten o'clock most of these kids think I'm some square white guy who works as a substitute teacher and they're right whatever happened to Al Capone who ate his macaroni al dente *The Hotel Wentley Poems* are as good as he thought today is John's birthday or was it yesterday Jim calls leaves a singing message Isabel phones can we come to dinner celebrate their wedding anniversary Mike phones says today is Wieners' birthday Amanda writes that Pinochet's brain attached to hers and her trip to the supermarket the lottery chatter how are the kids and beef stew people walk around in t-shirts and shorts the earth isn't right but I may be wrong a black boy at ballet thinks Julia and a half American half Korean boy are brother and sister Julia says he's not my brother well he looks like he should be the boy's mother is eating her third honey-dipped donut drinking an extra large coffee Celeste stretches her body alongside other girls on the studio floor turkey tacos for supper refried beans Julia says don't mind me I'm going to eat 'til I burst imagine you have flowers on your head instead of hair pick out five objects that interest you draw the sun and moon above Winter Hill opposite ends of Broadway seventh grade boy stands in the office eight-fifteen in the morning tall and fit with braided hair cinnamon skin hazel eyes baggy jeans long basketball shirt first pink slip of the day in hand waiting to see Mr. Williams he lives with his mother two brothers and sister in the projects he dreads having to be home to take care of the younger ones his mother works father not around nor any of the dad's of his siblings friends all want something from him girls all want something from him no one to trust teachers are behind him but the teachers live some place else and you have to leave them at the end of the school day this pink slip gets him an extra hour with them at the end of the day Deja is half Puerto Rican half Dominican lives up near Broadway with her mother and step father Deja's father has a business and makes good money and supports Deja and her sister Deja is envied at school because she dresses the latest styles is smart gets good grades until her stepfather starts doing inappropriate things with her Mark calls we'll do some recording on Wednesday night no I never heard back from Tony at PA's I missed a good reading with Gerrit and C.A. Conrad at Out of the Blue dinner with Michael and Isabel and Bill and Beverly Katha and Tom Patricia and Chris Ben and Judy soup good red wine Michael's grandmother's dumplings and roast chicken chocolate pudding just as I'm thinking there's no traffic I'll be at Mark and Melissa's farm in no time the car spits and pops the lights go out the car dies right there in the middle of the on-ramp to Route 2 high evening rush hour call Triple A call Molly call Mark sitting here waiting for a tow truck drivers struggle to get around me blowing horns yelling flashing fingers the tow truck driver has six kids works a day job he's thirty-two with two kids in high school Molly and the girls pick me up at the garage load my guitar and amp into Molly's shiny new Toyota back home pizza everyone is going to outline a character maybe it will be a character in the story you are going to write how long does it have to be Dick is a detective in a trench coat Waundel is a mulatto girl who lives with her mother and father her father is black and her mother is white I am angry and I hate the world and if you mess with me I will kill you think of your scenes like a movie what if you want to write about rape my sister takes my mother's car keys before the registry revokes her license two accidents this past week she insists she's a good driver been driving for a long time why are you doing this to me she wants to know you can't take my car I have a spotless record I have a spare key she says I'll use it so my brother-in-law pulls her coil wire someone with a big dog is leaving shit around the neighborhood now this morning without knowing it I stepped in something while walking Sparky tracked it into Molly's new Toyota driving Molly to the hospital back in the house through the living room into the kitchen onto the stool leg where I rested my foot while eating my toast Celeste Rice Crispies Julia chicken parm calzone what's that smell my car needs an alternator Molly's watching a French movie I'm making meatballs Celeste doesn't like gnocchi it's Julia's favorite she passes her Kung Fu test moves to a higher belt says she wants me to cook gnocchi to celebrate so I boil a separate pot and cook some angel hair for Celeste old lady at the café every day bumming cigarettes going into other stores bakery hair salon could I bum cigarette from you dear I have some but they're at home bowl of sauce in the fridge lots of meatballs feed off it for days breakfast is leftover gnocchi for Julia last of the angel hair for Celeste slice of toast for me two cups of coffee persons and places and things oh my rain then freezing temperatures tiny fish that eat the plant get eaten by bigger fish loons eat the fish mercury snowballs through the food chain growing to drastic proportions the water looks pristine but dangerous levels of Neil's not seeing his girlfriend any more she lives in Lawrence the travel undid them he has new teepees to put on his land she no teepee she has no car her friends have cars and there's a brand new senior citizens center in the town let's see what happens I want to get my eyes tested I think it's my eyes winter has finally arrived eight degrees at Logan Airport thousands in southern New Hampshire without power morning news powerless man and woman in winter coats and hats play Scrabble by candle light at their kitchen table leave a message for Gerrit how 'bout lunch next week spring session is already full twenty-five students two on the wait list eleven registered for the evening session things to do before end of break clean out bottom area of basement stairs get syllabi in order take Sparky to the vet for his teeth finish proofing *They Say* send *Call Me Waiter* to Bill mail *The Hotel Wentley Poems* to Ben Mazer clean kitchen cabinets and appliances work through pile miscellaneous papers on top of the microwave organize clothes and closets call pediatrician to get inhaler script for Julia's school nurse French bread at La Cascia for meatball subs take to the farm tonight recording with Mark gas car stop at store for dishwashing soap contact Janet at UMass change of a student's grade girls to school and back homework drop Julia off at Kung Fu wash load of my sweaters and sweatshirts find gloves Mike calls sorry to be out of touch work's been busy Derek emails happy new year how are things Deb is interested in using one of her images for *Call Me Waiter* cover eight o'clock morning sun not so low as a week ago this same time turn down Broadway from

Central Street a young woman at the bus stop tears
in her eyes Celeste writes I have a wonderful life in
her weekend journal the woman who works at the
café's driving license revoked she failed to pay a
speeding ticket in New Hampshire I thought it was
another state and I didn't have to worry mushroom
caps sprout Julia takes photos with her new camera
tacos savory greens chocolaty brownies Chinese
dumplings lasagna Grandmother's Cheesecake
Christmas cookies Spanish chicken fettuccine with
pears and Gorgonzola cheese the teacher's note
thanks us all for our contributions and she will try
all of the delicious recipes don't forget the kindness
journals due on the one-hundredth day of school
they want to create a mansion a huge mansion with
many rooms high ceilings lots of big windows wall
to wall carpets indoor and outdoor pool Jacuzzi huge
kitchen game room servants expensive furniture big
trees many flowers in the big yard a big screen tele-
vision big circular driveway skylights father's leaving
home and rape and fights between rival gangs drug
dealers and drug addicts breaking up with their
boyfriends a girl living in a foster home her siblings
living in a different foster home their mother in jail
father dead a detective on the trail of a serial killer a
high school boy who wants to be a baseball star a
student who is in the eighth grade who hates school
and teachers and dreams of being grown up and free

she cries into the phone wants to know why this is happening if she'd only had new glasses she wouldn't have the accidents it's not the end of the world I tell her she has friends with cars and the senior citizens van yes she can go to Florida and visit her older sister Bob phones tumor on Carol's spine emergency surgery tomorrow John Ashbery answers all of his interview questions with fewer than sixty words Charles Bernstein takes up to six hundred words and who is afraid of Ron Silliman temperature below zero Tom Brady and a woman's sports bra Bob says not to let my girls use iPods it will ruin their hearing take them to hear chamber music opera and children should wear uniforms be taught the basics of reading writing and math I phone the other Bob to see if March twenty-second works for him same for Mark and Melissa Dear Tony thanks for getting back again I'm old to be playing rock-and-roll I'm old to be the father of a ten- and seven-year-old at night awake for hours worrying what will happen if I die before they are adults Dear Mr. Torra I am writing to current and recent patients of my husband William sadly to inform you that on December 22 William died and for those of you not recently in touch I know this news will come as a great shock as it did for our family the therapist I saw at the time referred me to this eccentric psychiatrist who might help me with medication treatment this imposing oversize man with white head of hair wearing sandals no socks shorts unkempt office books stacked to the ceiling science novels history poetry philosophy one thing piled on the next says lots of poets are bi-polar like Roethke and James Wright but they didn't have the kinds of medication then I can help you if you're willing how long before I'll notice if it's going to work with this one you should notice some difference within a week the woman at the party says there's you're next novel the story of a man whose shrink died and he needs to find another it would be a best seller they'd make a movie didn't Woody Allen do that the list contains names and numbers of doctors who'll take my insurance I'm on the phone back and forth with the doctor's office and my insurance company setting up the approval for visits to the new doctor pressing two then three then pound then four to finally be put on official hold at the insurance company two separate times hard to do much yoga with the shoulder injury fish tacos ribs and the coconut macaroons wine the bartender is pouring some kind of new wave vodka thing with fruit McKinnon's Market four-and-a-half pound chicken a bag of carrots celery large onion and a box of noodles eight dollars thirteen cents Celeste home with a cold after all these years the doctor suddenly dies who saw me any time at his home office night or day Saturday or Sunday when I didn't have insur-

| 34 |

ance he said come anyway Amanda writes she's forced to make decisions for her mother and feeling guilty for stealing time away from her children to write about it she saw the poet and crossed the street to avoid him no time for poetry my mother says that she'll take the medication because she has been having a little loss of memory it's the same medication helped her years ago but she stopped taking it because of leg cramps I'd rather die than have one more night with those leg cramps grilled cheese sandwiches for Julia and Celeste's breakfast Julia still hungry bowl of leftover chicken soup bundle them up four degrees outside fifteen below with the wind can't keep the house warm Sparky outside quick shit piss back on the porch wants in next week appointments dentist physical therapy and new shrink how fast we must get on with it one minute you've got this guy you call and hang out and I always feared that one of the shaky piles of books would crash down upon me his theory that psychiatry in the twentieth century is a great scam we are just animals and it's all hard-wired from the beginning you can put a man in the monastery he'd say but you can't stop him from masturbating he drops dead couldn't be more than sixty-five or seventy why shouldn't I write a novel about a man whose shrink dies the tragic angle a man spinning deeper into his madness unable to obtain help and ends up

living in front of the Boston Public Library that's
what happens all the time says Molly Julia Celeste
Sparky and I ascend the trail up Pine Hill dusting of
snow ice balls collect on Sparky's paws Celeste and
Julia look for acorns top of the hill look down on
Interstate 93 out over Medford Somerville Charles-
town onto Boston's skyscrapers and the bridges Julia
takes photo of Celeste in front of the tower the old
twisted stunted tree by the frozen pond where two
boys shovel a place to skate bend over to help
Sparky with the ice balls my doctor died and I won-
der if you would be able to give me some medication
to get me through until I see my new doctor braised
short ribs with rice and spinach Julia eats leftovers
for breakfast Celeste scrambled eggs I went for a
hike with my Daddy Julia and Sparky we hiked up a
hill I could see Boston I found acorns on the ground
tomorrow Celeste has Word of the Day don't forget
snacks for the class her new word is thank you in
Chinese kid in her class says he hates Chinese
people because they are ugly another classmate tells
her she'll burn in hell if she doesn't believe in God
Celeste wants to know why don't we believe in
God and the girl in her class will pray for her soul
three fire trucks lights blink and twirl traffic backs
to the McGrath Highway in a matter of minutes one
lane open on Highland Avenue cut down the alley
drive down the one-way of Oxford to our driveway

Virgies is a Highland Ave. neighborhood joint cater-
ing to postal workers and local tradesmen bad bar
food pool table darts and Keno after the facelift it's
Madison's On The Ave. no more Bud sign new sign
says nightly dinner specials I remember a time when
I was in high school Davis Square so desolate a Mac-
Donald's went out of business some people believe
in God and some people don't and even the people
who believe in God don't all believe in the same God
like Jesus Celeste wants to know yes like Jesus no
perversion no transgression care in solitude this is
how to live I have a long way to go over the Zakim
through the tunnel to UMass Boston did you have a
good vacation I didn't know I was on a vacation
never got to the bottom of the basement stairs the
class is full if you are not on the electronic wait list
you don't have much chance to get into the class
Frost Williams Bishop Wieners Kerouac Morrison
Welty Faulkner Amanda writes why it matters to be
remembered what value in the old objects you find
cleaning out a desk memories glued to them
cherries soaked in her grandmother's Manhattans
her father's voice the stain in the carpet left by the
boiler repairman's boot Sam at her breast who won't
remember this her moment that matters statue of a
Chinese Buddha wearing sunglasses gift from
Celeste on top of big blue dictionary that Molly
bought me on a birthday when I was in college real

fur on your hat yes rabbit approved Brazilian church
on Highland Ave. bell tower wrapped in scaffolding
same church I wrote about a hawk perched on the
steeple's cross to prey on lesser birds same church
once was the Somerville Boxing Club Maureen says
I don't have to come any more my arm has improved
keep doing the exercises at home ok to light yoga
the new shrink gives me a prescription come every
month in the beginning then every other month my
therapist says see you in two weeks more light in the
day now Sparky's claws scrawl across the living room
floor above me Celeste brings worksheets home for
homework over Broadway gray clouds hover all the
way down to Charlestown and Boston top of the
Bunker Hill Monument shrouded nobody gives you
a break if you need to turn from Central St. onto
Broadway my mother was a looker in her shy and
quiet way there's a lady she met at the senior citi-
zen's center what's her name now I can't remember
her name and my friend Mary who works in a real
estate office she doesn't sell many houses maybe
one or two a year but it keeps her busy will drop by
later she still drives her own car we'll go out for cof-
fee it's the place we always go I put poison out to kill
the mice smell of dead flesh Mike and I agree this is
the worst band we've ever seen drop Bill off after our
meeting four boxes of books to sell put them in the
back of my wagon use the money for Pressed Wafer

straighten living room and kitchen take Celeste to ballet go to market for groceries Julia wants a Scrabble game make a stop at Target the mind of Tao is deep and hard to fathom two o'clock in the morning unable to sleep myriad worries toss from side to side in the dark try not to watch the clock fifty descriptions of a place pace myself four maybe five at a time pay attention to the details I tell them at least two or three paragraphs can it be a kind of state of mind place she wants to know Hey Joe Mark and I can play Monday or Tuesday night next week but I don't think Bob can do either of those nights Amanda at the Grande Café Union Square Sunday mornings with all the male poets arguing poetics and dreadfully much else she sat on the sofa giggling to herself knitting I haven't talked with Frank since he hung up on me for saying what I said about his wife pregnant weekend weather woman predicts coldest spell this year still no snow I have nothing against punctuation I simply don't know where to put it right now Molly has three patients who hit her while she is trying to give them medication two of them have a stomach virus shit and puke the bed round the clock new shrink's nothing like the old clean cut suit and tie shoes shined orderly office what brings you here my old shrink died suddenly Tommy Lee Jones holds me captive underground enormous aquariums fish of all shapes and sizes swimming inside them Tommy Lee says I'll eat poison snail before he's through with me I escape speeding down a winding road in a car that suddenly spins out of control drive over the edge into the sea one of the workmen found a dead rat out there I saw him toss it over into the bushes it's finally too cold for the people in the house behind us they took the party indoors my old neighbor who died had a phone in the screen house during the summer it would ring day and night they didn't use an answering machine when they were out it rang for minutes at a time extra layers of clothes in the morning warm the car up for twenty minutes student's mother on a life support system not expected to survive she's staying in school no matter what happens can I give her some future assignments should she have to take time off another student's mother just died that's why she wasn't here first week of class what do I have to do to catch up the freeze is on I sit alone in the house furnace working overtime somewhere on Berkeley Street a car alarm goes off math story problems for Celeste then some reading dead frozen sparrow on the sidewalk outside the kids' school Celeste wants to bury it the ground is frozen the waitress won't shut up about her father who had Alzheimer's Disease she pronounces it Alltimers how crazy he became my mother listens intently nodding her head says well now they have medicine the waitress

pays her no mind the last year before he died I had
to watch him eat he'd forget to swallow his food so
she had to sit there and keep reminding him to swal-
low so he wouldn't choke but she wasn't going to let
him die in a nursing home after breakfast I ask my
mother where she wants to buy her Kleenex I don't
need to go to the store she says but on the way to
breakfast you said you needed Kleenex oh no not
today the new neighbors cut down the old neigh-
bor's peach tree trunk and branches cut and piled
neatly next to their outdoor fire pit subway train
over the Longfellow Bridge river freezing over
patches of purple blue clouds against pink dusk sky
Citgo sign flashes above Kenmore Square excuse me
he says standing over me holding the upper handle
has anyone ever talked to you about Jesus I'm read-
ing Derek's new poems when I should be reading
student work I've stopped working as a substitute
teacher until further notice Amanda writes about
knitting row after row punching holes James and the
kids asleep the wind whipping around outside their
house is cold pregnant weatherwoman First Alert
Doppler temperatures should be climbing I haven't
done any laundry this week we need groceries
Celeste says she's sad about the dead bird sign up
for parent teacher conferences make appointment
for Sparky's teeth cleaning next week Chinese New
Year you can wear out your brain trying to make

things into one without realizing that they are all the same the Taoists call this Three In The Morning now I have written something I don't know whether what I have written really says something or whether it hasn't said something Chuang Tzu writes don't try to help life along and knowledge has limitations six plus six will always be twelve and the big pines I study from the kitchen window sway what is the point of writing a poem if you are not going to write it in poetic form but whose form is it I want clean air for my children but we have two cars and heat our house with gas buy products shipped by truck and rail Sparky wakes me jumps up to sleep by my side ambulance front of the old neighbor's house they bring her out in a stretcher load her into the back of the ambulance drive away the solstices are different depending on which side of the hemisphere we ride The Great Clod burdens me with form too I found out who's leaving the large poops around the neighborhood the thirty-something woman who lives a few houses down with the Lab this morning the divine squat dropping one in a neighbor's driveway she made no effort to pick it up my past is riddled with mistakes ache my mind won't let go had I the ability to separate myself from the past maybe I'm wrong saying there are no rules for plot and character in ancient times this was called Freedom of the Bound Dear Joe I'm kind of stuck with my writing I was wondering if I could sit in on a couple of your classes Dear Elise you could but it would be redundant how about going to look at art see a good movie listen to music find poets you like and read everything you can get your hands on by them maybe go to some poetry readings first storm this winter not much snow more freezing rain and sleet down fast and hard stings the face accidents all over town surfaces icing over fresh snow from this morning's now weighted down rain sodden Julia and I shovel out to the street and clear a space for one of the cars Ange says writing about yourself is a boring proposition no Mommy Poet she wants to contribute something to the world that it's never seen and therefore viscerally opposed to autobiography heavy snow rain and ice collapse the new neighbor's screen house what did they think would happen of they left it up Molly wants to know my joy and anger prevail throughout the four seasons what if I contribute something to the world that has never been seen and nobody sees it the next passage will be boring because I tell you about how two days ago I put a full load of kids' clothes in the dryer and two of the girls' bed quilts in the washer and I forgot them because I've been so busy the bed quilts have been sitting wet in the washer big fish little fish and when man becomes distraught he kills you can read all about it in the book she says she's sorry to miss so many classes but she wants to get back on track he hasn't been here the last two weeks because he thought he dropped the course but it turns out he didn't so he wants to take it Michael Franco walks down the icy sidewalk snow spikes strapped to leather shoes that look handmade in 1643 long cape and woolen hat Oxford Street meets Roanoke Chinese New Year Year of the Pig birds note the passing in tweets and whistles rustling about in the pine trees let the kids do what they will tonight soup dumplings pork crispy fish tofu with exotic mushrooms noodles vegetables fried ice cream tea and Chinese no matter how hot-tempered a man seeking revenge shouldn't smash his enemy's sword words aware of nothing but sparrow wings and songs birds sing standing on one leg Tree stance breathe in and out slowly switch legs down on my back face up on floor breathe into the stomach out gently through the nose grilled turkey and cheese sandwich for Julia cereal for Celeste snap crackle and pop our ears down at the bowl Box session we run through the set the kids running in and out Melissa's lasagna Bob's spinach pie Avery Veronica Julia and Celeste perpetual adventure wake up sore throat head cold I won't be coming up today I've got a cold and sore throat you've got to take care of yourself she says but at least you sound good though I can hardly speak Mike emails live performance MC5 Wayne

State University 1970 Wayne Cramer is Master Lai who said The Great Clod Burdens Me With Form Master Lai also says if you value your life you must therefore value your death the same lady walks in the café and bums a smoke trying to nap fatigue from this sore throat hammering and banging when we moved in three siblings lived there for decades one of the brothers died before I got to know them the sister got sick with cancer stopped me on the street to tell me about her latest surgery how they took all her insides she has to go to the bathroom in a plastic bag then there's only the one brother in that big single family shingles and roof rotting back porch caved in then one day I realize I haven't seen the last brother for months next there's a for sale sign followed by the work crew portable potty demolish the porch and stairs convert to two family condos toss and turn in and out of light sleep low grade fever scratchy cough now the tooth that recently had a root canal broke students ask why care Frank O'Hara wears underwear or not they don't know who Lady Day is show them Lady Day's singing "Strange Fruit" on Youtube haven't been to the laundry pile for a week my mother phones what time are you coming today I'm not coming today I was supposed to come two days ago but I was sick oh I didn't know you were sick but you sound good temperature rising the last few days ice in driveway and sidewalks melts water streams down the street sewers overflow celebrity checked herself in and out of rehab three times England has a plan for withdrawing its troops sports guy says Manny hasn't shown up for spring training claims his mother is ill but he's spotted at an antique auto show Jim reads at the Plough and Stars his wife punched a guy in the face here years ago people at the bar talk while Jim reads some of us are there for the reading others because it's Sunday night and they've been drinking all day February the new neighbors plant shrubs where they filled in the old neighbor's fish pond they're standing inside the roofless half-collapsed screen house drinking beer Spanish music blasting cases of empty beer bottles pile up sauté ginger onions mushrooms and spinach serve over brown rice I found lyrics I wrote last year though I never put them to music and now I know why they're not very good the bear that growls is grating a lame excuse for saying it is the same game I'm holding on sitting on the rug patting the dog finally cleaning out the bottom of the basement stairs straighten my studio organize school papers and top of desk trash bag full from stuff on the floor she finishes the root canal instructs me two to three weeks begin work on post and crown Thursday second visit with the new shrink today file the letter about the old shrink dropping dead been sitting on top of my desk every

day on television the news stories and film-footage
new Japanese Red Sox pitcher shopping golfing eat-
ing walking leaving the locker room with his cute
interpreter by his side my mother says her friend
told her she could take a test and get her license
back after she gets new glasses if she could see bet-
ter she wouldn't have bumped those cars my father
had problems she said but he didn't do anything real
bad Amanda writes about Tuesday and how every-
where she turns things are building up there's more
to do more choices to make one of James's students
told him he would be dead within two weeks and he
was all the heavy rain floods the tot lot the big news
for the kids getting out from school who gather
around the little pond some wade in slowly not to
let the water over the tops of their rain boots others
plunge in knee deep frantic mothers' calls get out of
the water fall on deaf airs Celeste finds a dead bird
on the front porch most of its head gnawed away
Daddy what did that it's so warm and sunny after
the heavy rains open the skylight like spring
though early March layers of ice and snow cling to
golden brown ground-stuff brush and bushes
grasses and gravel men's night in Derek Ryan Mike
James and Jim venison sausage with vinegar peppers
and wild mushrooms braised beef over cheesy rice
and salad eight bottles of wine half a bottle of bour-
bon talk about Amanda Amanda this and Amanda

that and religion and kids and how long should we read for at the Bootstrap reading and Jim sneaks up on a fly scoops it up places it in his mouth presents it on the tip of his tongue before swallowing I play Bob Kaufman you can hear his gums flap like part of the music changes take place I cannot determine their sources girls and I walk to the Asian market in Union Square tofu scallions Chinese cooking wine dried mushrooms look at the fish crabs fish heads rock candy for Molly sugar treats for the girls chilly breeze down Summer Street sun closer higher in the sky I'm good at recognizing the faults in others the greedy speedily drive exquisite cars down special lanes somehow in the middle of winter flies are hatching in the house no matter how many we kill there's twice as many Amanda writes apples left too long in the car pockmarked and uneatable I just ate an overripe banana people always say things that hurt other people some of those people don't know they are doing it or can't help themselves or didn't mean it the way it was interpreted or maybe want to say things that hurt people sometimes I feel I'm part of the world other times I feel withdrawn but I do regret when I make an error one pile of student poems now another two loads of kids laundry done now one load of mine followed by towels and a load of whites tofu with scallions broccoli and noodles wake at midnight unable to get back to sleep read

Pynchon television blonde women huge implants
grind each other on a pool table below zero outside
wind batters anything not fastened down loose gut-
ters rattle trash cans turn over pine trees mournful
wooooosh like the dead calling fall back asleep
around four dream Mike and I rowing on a lake with
a young boy who's Mike's son water so clear the sun
penetrates deep around large boulders and ledges
that make up the lake bottom suddenly the boat is
taking on water soon we're sinking I feel the boat go
out from under me look back at Mike but he's smil-
ing he just played a trick on me Gerrit phones leaves
a message I phone him leave a message he phones
me I answer he fills me in all the news and gossip
that's fit what book I am reading what twenty he
reads and I miss him he misses me who left a wine
mustard sauce on the stove the kids both up at six
in the morning today Celeste wants to wear torn
pants to school the ones Molly picked make her look
stupid sitting on the edge of her bed crying some
students grow uneasy when I tell them that poetry
doesn't have to make sense Julia and I fish in the
little pond I catch a fish but while reeling it in a croc-
odile attacks the fish then jumps up on shore tries
to bite my leg Sparky barks suddenly crocodiles
everywhere one snaps its jaws on Sparky but the
crocodile turns out to be a snake Julia starts scream-
ing and I wake up with my heart pounding awake

for two and a half hours list of things to be done turning over in my head fall back asleep Molly the girls and I at the Museum of Science but it's not Boston out into the garage to the car my father suddenly appears with a baseball bat attacks me we struggle over the bat I get hold of it strike him continually in the head call him a fucking asshole when the police arrive he claims that I attacked him temperature up to fifty degrees people walk around in t-shirts and shorts heating bill for the month of February up close to four hundred dollars Amanda writes about omens in the night flags flap against metal flagpoles bone found in a graveyard it will be seven to ten years before they bring the Green Line into Union Square where twenty years ago in Sal's Italian Kitchen I watched Sal and his family get into a fistfight son slugging it out with Sal the mother hitting the son the daughter throwing coffee cups during the breakfast rush you can't stay in love in a dream no matter how hard you try a mouse trap exists because the mouse is not like the stock market or a race won it's more about shades of gray not black and white snow with a summer bee ice in the driveway water seeps into the basement mice scamper in the ceiling could I serve on the PTA for one more term there's no one else who wants the position read poetry with third graders Tuesday at ten he quits the class because Frank O'Hara is a homo another student yet to attend appears mid-semester any way I can catch up biggest snow storm this winter week before first day of spring now heavy rain nearly a foot of slush slowly shovel my way out to the street heart speeding sweaty soaked in the downpour top of the driveway three-foot packed wall pushed up by city plows my heart sinks toughest work's ahead suddenly a teenage boy shovel over shoulder turns the corner from School on to Oxford I'll do that for you how much how much will you give me tell me how much you think is fair twenty he says looks at me like he expects me to bargain okay do a good job and he does while I shovel out the back walk and back porch and clean the cars I pay him and he's off in his drenched jacket and sneakers hair dripping wet Celeste doesn't want to go to ballet says she's glad I'm her father Rice Crispies her breakfast of choice for the month running Julia fried egg sautéed spinach eggs Molly home sick coughing sneezing achy the birds disrupted display displeasure at the weather from tree to tree sassy songs branches weighed down wet snow pine tree boughs bow in the middle right now is the moment I've lived for and anything from here on out is a gift be content with it the book says fate has been decided for me enough to have the feelings of a man and the things I choose opposed to the things I choose not to freezing temps glaze yesterday's rain Sunday morning Julia and I drive to Bella in South Medford mother Bella and her two middle-aged sons who still live at home two pounds cheese ravioli that's all there is to it is a potentially loaded statement the master who went around saying that's all there is to it started the That's All There Is To It movement and people continued to follow it for nearly three months don't expect too much from the world if you fight the current you will drown old wood catches the moss from the north side of the tree where it's not the only place it grows and all I have to say when they approach with inquiries is that's all there is to it and when I die sky blue trades in fields of praise Dear Christine no I won't be reading any late work during my vacation Molly still sick Celeste getting sick big pot of chicken noodle soup the furnace in Amanda and James's house died it will cost four thousand dollars Sparky scratches a lot I think he's got flees the furnace kicks in tonight vernal equinox forty degrees stranger in the café interrupts my conversation home schooling is stupid mastering technique doesn't cut it but to dissolve the duality between myself and the breadcrumbs add to ground turkey eggs grated cheese salt pepper fresh parsley and basil roll into meatballs brown then simmer in tomato sauce serve over penne side of spinach Julia's been eating from the pot of chicken soup for three days late breakfast with Bill at Charlie's on Columbus Ave. ham steak eggs home fries Bill says his grandsons don't do Disney too below them Bob phones Carol in the hospital at least three more weeks he spoke yesterday at BU shocked that students had not heard of Sacco and Vanzetti most of the snow melted bright clear March morning the First Alert Doppler calls for temperatures dropping tonight possibility of several inches of wet snow plump pregnant robins hop about the ground on fence-tops and flit from branch to branch the area around the house needs to be cleaned pick up the litter old weeds dried leaves and beat-up kids' toys Mike phones Cheetah Chrome Unnatural Axe The Nervous Eaters and Classic Ruins the Linwood on April fourth Celeste wakes runs down the stairs wants her breakfast be up in a minute I've got one more minute to write must finish reading proofs then twenty-five short story drafts my studio chilly tips of my toes cold take Celeste to ballet Sparky treat with anti-flea medicine sometimes I daydream about moving away somewhere where I don't know one person for miles and miles but after three weeks there is no barrier between inside and outside that's why I can hear the birds now Julia in PA's Lounge reads the newspaper on a stool at the bar drinking soda laughing at Paul Violi's funny poems Dan and Derek and Bill Joel Dave and Lisa hello hello what you been up to and John from the Out of the Blue reading series there too I'm tired of poetry readings there have been hundreds over the years but it's good to see friends and if the reading is boring I can think about what I will cook for supper Amanda still no word so I re-read what she's already written but I can't find the beef stew recipe I miss my Gloucester friends how long since I did the 128 mole to Cape Ann visit Gerrit Amanda Patrick James walk Stage Fort Park or Ravenswood maybe run into Willie Alexander on Main Street if you look for something in front of you it will sneak up behind then you're left standing in some old overcoat sullen in the rain I miss you Walt Whitman wrestling trees how long Ginsberg gone who sits on the edge of high peak clouds and mountains secure in sacred hut close enough for shelter the signal that the dryer cycle is finished goes on too long an annoying grind more than ring I am afraid that if I don't rush around madly from sunrise to sunset in order to achieve and accumulate then the ones who do will be better off than I another dead bird how many this winter Julia asks holding my hand we cross Highland Ave. on our way to Kung Fu the teacher said fuck sestinas and villanelles my mother puts her eyeglasses away I don't need these what do you mean you don't need those you can't see without them no I don't only sometimes if I'm reading and having a little trouble but you've been wearing them for years Joe don't tell me I've been around a long time Celeste sees the morning moon hiding beneath restless charcoal clouds what will happen about my daughters after I am gone funeral procession north on the Fellsway car after car little death-flags on the roof sun and moon opposite horizons my mother races down the street trying to run me over driving an old brown Buick I run up on the sidewalk she follows back onto the street then over a walkway she's still in pursuit down a dead end alley my back against a fence what are you doing you're going to kill me she's inches away racing the engine shouting in English but I hear it in tongues wearing a stylish brown leather jacket her hair is long flowing furious with me screaming the girl in the café says she wants to be in a band but doesn't play anything she's been jamming with a friend who's in a band that just got signed Affirmative Fryer so that's really cool her friend plays guitar she's played drums a few times not really she doesn't know how she just bangs on all the different things but it sounds pretty cool Julia home from school with a stomach bug Celeste argues over changing her shirt too small no it isn't Daddy next three weeks overdrive forty-five short stories two final projects the African drum music throbs from inside the blue house in the summer they party through the night speakers blasting from the patio Sunday's first meeting of the garden col-

lective on Prospect Hill plant seeds clean garden
check compost make long- and short-term plans with
fellow gardeners sometimes I think it feels good to
get depressed thinking I haven't been treated fairly
taxes need to be done along with six loads of laun-
dry kitchen floor is filthy downstairs bathroom quick
wet mop kitchen floor sweep front patio pick up
debris pack last's years weeds that crunch apart in
my hands into yard waste bag Amanda writes Abi-
gail finally getting better she's feeding her with a
tube now how her house smells like a burnt out old
car and when you toss a stone skips along the water
until it stops and drops Julia turns eleven doesn't
want a cake but hot fudge sundaes Molly and Julia
at Staples for printer cartridges Celeste out on the
patio playing with the dirt in the big plant pots a
good completion it is written takes a long time not
what's stylish Celeste calls me to the window to see
a red cardinal skip along the top of the neighbor's
fence then the female more brown than red appears
old neighbor taken away in a stretcher has returned
sitting in the wheelchair on her front porch blanket
wrapped around her legs so shriveled all head ready
to fall off her children swarm the three-decker wait-
ing on the mother waiting and waiting on her to die
but she won't it's been at least two years she's dying
by the end of the week but as if to defy the daugh-
ters plotters in selling off everything the old lady

owns she keeps a life-line the new neighbors behind
us finally cleaned the yard threw all the empty cases
of beer away still no roof on the screen house my
being slips into non-being being that I've gained a
foot and now want to hold on to it I think the good
doctor Williams was right when he wrote that it's the
hours we keep to see things makes all the difference
down Oxford Street Michael's car still in driveway
past gossipy Cathy who's got some passerby caught
in her grip while Britney the bulldog wrestles with a
rubber ball and the garbage truck's got traffic stuck
the men toss bags and barrels driver beeps the horn
behind me until the garbage man waves us around
and I saw the neighborhood kids rushing to the con-
venience store junk food for the day make it to
school before the bell and the teachers with their
heavy school bags oversize coffee cups and the Goth
rock chick unlocking the porn store door and the
worn faces of day laborers huddled at Broadway and
McGrath long slow line traffic onto the Expressway
four lanes down to one onto the ramp flag flying
high over the Schraff's Building who knows the
Expressway as I do knows Medford yields to
Somerville along the Mystic River Somerville gives
way to Cambridge west sprawl of scaffold construc-
tion new hotels and office buildings then to the east
red clumsy three-decker and redbrick Charlestown
hills Breeds and Bunker the battle at Breeds the

monument on Bunker and the Mystic River Bridge reaching across the sky behind a jet departs Logan glint of sun Boston Stone and Gravel First and Finest and the masts of the U.S.S. Constitution steeple of the Old North Church above North End rooftops and the gulls hang in air pockets above the Zakim Bridge Boston Garden I will always call it and Spalding Rehabilitation my father's dead eyes look up before the doctor closes them and pulls the sheet over old Hancock's shadow on the new Hancock down into the tunnel and the three men in a white pickup truck fuck you out the window they think I cut them off end of tunnel big trucks rumble out into daylight pass Southie Mass. Ave. smokestacks the old Bickfords the Boston Globe building to Columbia Point and you tired students walking the long seaside walkway along white-capped Dorchester Bay in time we everyone look up from under the sheet I mean to bring a poem to you a poem you will understand what good is it to me if you can't understand it but you've got to try hard but cold raw temps First Alert Doppler predicts warm next week we'll even see the sun local news still abuzz new Red Sox pitcher teaching viewers Japanese words I'll write it here another 'copter down a snooping bear causing problems in western suburbs after the break she thinks her old neighbor died another old neighbor is on bed rest and how she's not certain whether

she should be doing more or doing less and her
head feels fuzzy says she hates those who question
her decisions Bill calls Pressed Wafer party for Ed's
and Taylor's new books but that's Mother's Day two
students agitated something one said about the
other's poem it's my poem and I can write what I
want but simply writing your opinions is not a poem
it is if it's my poem Celeste quits ballet returns to
Kung Fu on the way to school says Daddy did I tell
you I know how to make the blues no you didn't
how do you make the blues I don't feel like telling
you right now smell garbage and sewage low tide
gulls skulk on the ground or circle above the mud
flats I ask how far she wants to walk oh I love to walk
I'll walk as far as you want I let her talk try to listen
she orders shrimp with vegetables eats in tiny bites
talks sentences she can't finish likes this place it's
clean third and fourth grade poetry group haiku
count the beats silly haiku serious haiku nature
haiku spring haiku sports haiku group haiku boys
goofing in the corner no haiku the master said trans-
mit the established facts not words of exaggeration
and if you do that you'll probably come out all right
Celeste says she doesn't like gray mornings why
don't you write one book with a Hollywood ending
my new shrink asks then you could make a million
and be happy to write the books you want to write
why doesn't he mind his own fucking business the

snake moves only with its back bone and ribs but manages to get along will you come join us in the first step of our child's salvation r.s.v.p. if you focus too much on the outside you'll suffer on the inside we need a bigger house Molly says not enough room here brown mixed pork veal and beef sauté garlic add tomatoes paste salt pepper fresh basil fresh parsley toss in the ground meat simmer down two hours serve over ziti with green salad I shoot Yul Brynner with a James Bond pen-gun right through the back he turns lunges for me I empty the pen on him he's down on a knee I pick up a knife plunge hard down through his skull hailstone storm destroys a massage parlor in Viet Nam Funeral Parlor the table inside a chain restaurant inside a shopping mall at Christmas a bar movie theater by all means have one of the senior citizens drown in fake butter after falling into the popcorn machine and an army truck out on the desert at night New York City Southie an island in Buzzard's Bay a dungeon in medieval times a boxing ring kitchen hotel room in a car en route to a town in a college classroom in a women's shoe store at a party in the hood on a fishing boat subway train at abandoned church prune raspberry bushes cut dead branches trim back the green turn soil then fill buckets with new compost spread over freshly turned soil begin pile for next year's compost coffee pizza talk of the hawk who feeds on the squirrels

who feed on our vegetables Celeste playing an elec-
tronic game Julia naps on the sofa Molly working at
the hospital too much laundry to face kitchen floor
filthy living room to be vacuumed downstairs bath-
room dirty again the dishwasher shifts to rinse cycle
pads of Sparky's feet beat time on the floor in the
café Neil sips his espresso says people are stupid
there's no other way to explain why they think the
way they think in sleep go visiting awake hustle I
get entangled unable to forget the distinctions police
siren Highland Ave. Plough and Stars Bill reads
Lowell Wieners his own poems old and new how do
you introduce Corbett John wants to know Julia says
without him knowing Molly says the cost of living
in Portland is thirty-five percent less and we could
make the same money thirty-three dead shooting
spree at a university gunman takes his own life I
missed Gerrit on the radio some poems have the
form of poetry but not the feeling of poetry maybe
I'm kidding myself pigeons gulls sparrows flock in
their own sections of Foss Park my father and I in
the basement of the old Medford house I see why
you wanted this space he says pointing to corner I
used to clear out for my own play area we chase the
funeral procession through the streets of the North
End unable to catch up three hours awake read Pyn-
chon toss and turn fall back to sleep around four up
at six coffee pack Molly's lunch local news when will

the rain end are our local colleges safe Julia naps
Celeste on the computer Sparky sleeping the eaves
rattle in the wind the house shifts with the planet's
pitch there is more to be learned but I have no room
left I forget my feet in those comfortable shoes if I
reject conventional values I must reject the conven-
tional values of words Ramones poster flaps when
heat blows through the vent how will this affect the
spirits and demons out with the old in with the new
been used for thousands of years this is what is
called out with the old and in with new eight bags
of groceries we're sure stocked up now Dad Roland
Kirk video in the classroom this is like poetry
Williams interview we are not English don't speak
English don't speak iambic pentameter clean out
your ears and listen sunshine blue sky fifty-five
degrees workmen scaffold the house behind us Julia
and Celeste take Sparky for a walk to the corner and
back don't talk to any strangers Bob anarchist Bob
phones help him get Carol up the stairs in her
wheelchair the universe is not humane Baby
Boomers returning to the church tonight at eleven
this God is in his fifties balding pony-tail gray hair
and a vest please don't be waiting for me is a great
lyric I wish I could admit punk is dead please arrive
by seven-thirty to toast the Irish poet what's his
name today is Thursday I left my car in the street
fifty dollar parking ticket I hope the better weather

curbs the crazy driving my dental insurance is used up for the year next week my crown and post will run around three hundred my new shrink gives too much advice close it and give me the script tie dead tree-trimmings in bundles dig holes for lettuce mix lime plant lettuce build pole structure for pole beans plant broccoli parsnips herb bushes from last year stored in pots at Taylor's house erect greenhouse Buddhist monks in a street brawl punching kicking and knocking each other to the ground the ones in orange robes get the best of it we walk to the library Celeste's first library card the girls check out books stop at the park the kids play Molly and I bask in warmth on a bench it seems like the winter would never end she says again the old lady in the three-decker taken away in an ambulance one of her daughters by her side die you old thing I know the daughter's thinking but the old lady will return she wants to change her major from elementary education to theater arts her parents help her with tuition they'd be disappointed if she didn't take her degree in something practical I want to get away she says I just want to get away today clip of Pollock painting and talking about his process he writes an imitation Williams poem attacking Williams anyone can do this poetry it's simplistic his father writes plays and prefers Yeats how horrible it is that a guy who lived in her apartment building got run over by a truck

and died while riding his bike got caught under the
rear wheels the car in the garage how much it will
cost make it three in a row and why does an old man
in Maine keep getting phone calls for Brad Pitt it's
confusing when a regular anchor or meteorologist
has a fill-in forsythia tulips jonquils dogwood daf-
fodils buds buds buds outside in the schoolyard
sound of cars on the Expressway seagulls hovering
red-brick housing projects bushes litter trees ready-
ing to leaf birds hop on branches red cars blue cars
gray cars black cars trucks and busses smokestacks
of power plant Mystic River water shiny the bridge
over the river dumpster overloaded man walks to his
car opens the door gets in starts the car drives away
squirrel hurrying up a tree trunk scared by the kids
I don't know what to write just write what you see
and hear but that's not a poem it's just a list why
can't a list be a poem because it can't om this is
Gerrit please leave a message turkey meatloaf riga-
toni with broccoli meatloaf sandwich for Julia this
morning Celeste cereal me whole grain toast with
peanut butter two cups coffee dishes in washer work
on laundry vacuum living room take out trash when
knowledge is allowed to take over there is a diffi-
culty in the mind I will never read through the
stacks of books on my desk does that mean I will
never read *The Confidence Man* again Dear Joe it's
amazing how class plays out in lit especially working

class lit it feels like you're somehow not supposed to do it that you're supposed to learn how to write up my computer's down I write this on Molly's Amanda writes that it is warming girls walk scantily clad drunks make their way home choosing which life she wants awake alone seeing clearly mistake foghorn for train how sound trades places peas coming up and going to the ocean Fu is when something returns to its origin on the premise that everything must return to its origin lone rower on the glassy bay distant Boston skyline Blue Hills farther out so nice today she says there used to be a lot of the older men you'd see walk here but they're gone same at the dances all the guys are gone now there's a couple of new ones but they're young and they don't even know the dances I don't tell them how old I am one time I was with your sister and a big dog chased us right here did I tell you that Aunt Gloria called and she wants me to go to Florida in August immortality can only be realized through long-term fasting and meditation so immortality is not in my future there are five movers five shakers five senses five relationships five corpses five types of contaminated energy and you must eliminate them all clear brush pile it high to be burned fill dumpster with old dock we demolished hot dogs on the grill for the kids the lake at night in mist you can't see the mountain Julia says all of us huddled on the shore the kids play on

and on in their childhood weekend past midnight
until they one by one slip into coma sleep Julia says
Celeste is supposed to listen to her Celeste says just
because Julia is older it doesn't mean she has to lis-
ten to her she kicked me no I didn't she pushed me
and called me an idiot no I didn't I told her she
couldn't use my Game Boy and she used it no sir she
told me I could use it no I didn't no I didn't she's a
liar she always lies and you always believe her she
gets to do anything she wants and you always
believe her she wouldn't help when I cleaned up the
room I told you I was going to help but you did it
before I could help liar liar I'm not going to the gar-
den if she's going fine then I won't go well maybe
none of us should go transplant lettuce and onions
water herbs beans lettuce and broccoli the plants
inside the greenhouse sluggish weather's been cold
weed raspberry bushes bursting green leaves cherry
and peach trees flowering first lilacs breaking
through along the lower terrace coffee pizza Emily
Scott Taylor Michelle Helen Dana Celeste and both
Julia covered in dirt talk of garden and bees dying
bad fathers bad academia bad weather bad wine bad
bread bad movies why not plan our first pot luck it'll
get to eighty this week Dear Professor Torra I know
that I've missed three weeks of class but I've had a
lingering cold I think this poem sucks I'm tired of
these people who trash this country like it's the

worst country in the history of civilization who does Ginsberg think he is God or something grapevine buds bust open tiny violet flowers if you measure by inches you'll be off by the time you reach ten feet electric saw slices through planks that fall onto plywood floors every day workmen put in ten-hour days our porch dilapidated gutters gone plumbing and electric need tending I can't even replace the hose for the kitchen sink-sprayer yesterday packed old videos in four boxes stored them in the basement even though we will never watch one again storage closet overflowing with things we never use store it all in the basement Harvard Square is Faggot Square Central Square is Niggerville and he'll punch out the face of the Chink if he crosses his line the Chinese man gets up and walks to the other end of the car that's just what I thought he'd do he says and who the fuck are you looking at you fucking faggot I'll knock that smile off of your face stick my head out at MGH stop no security he threatens an old lady who says why the nerve of you train full no where he lashes out at a young man calls him faggot off at Park Street to make Green Line connection can't find security person before the train takes off they say if you see something say something but to say something you need somebody to say something to teach class on my way back at Park Street stop he's standing there I walk down the line and board the last car in the train the Way has no artifice and no form Sun Ra said pay attention to the planets Celeste wakes in the middle of the night bad dream I fall back to sleep Celeste has a new pet part snake part turtle it's really a snake in a turtle shell wiggles out of the house I chase it down the driveway it loses its shell scurries off down the street too fast for me but all in slow motion Taylor's and Ed's new books Jim phones tells me about a woman in his office how does one understand how people act and what nature does Dear Joseph you are overdue for your blood check Dear Sparky time for your annual vet appointment Dear Joe will you mentor one of our new MFA students next fall First Alert Doppler got it wrong when they said sunny near eighty I sent Celeste out in t-shirt and light jacket it's cold raw and windy and she's in the Blue Hills on a field trip to visit the weather station he came to chew up your language and produce that is not in season should be avoided if you see him say hello he might be in Medford Square he stopped talking to me months ago because of what I said about his wife pizza for Julia scrambled eggs Celeste brush teeth and hair check homework take vitamins finish juice and who left the cap off the milk Amenoff's new paintings brilliant colors prehistoric figures geological forms rivers lakes and oceans into another returning to chaos necessary precondition for any new creation a long-tailed demon ram's horns out the side of his head reptilian webs for hands scales for skin it's only your animal ancestor right here it says Shadow Time many possible alternatives or parallel universes implies all time past present future as one time with infinite possible times next to that is written KEY chicken salad greens ice cream and bread thirty-two bucks the cashier gives her daughter fifteen thousand dollars a year towards college it's only a matter of time before they close the Beacon Street market managers talk great pitching he was burning that hill Amanda writes that her mother's medication is helping a little has my mother tried medication yesterday's rain falls on hanging laundry tried to call got as far as dialing the number the air smells like rain and earth May Day girls dance in white slight turn of events and you're stuck in ancient times everything green trees fully leaved yellow pollen dust settles on cars streets and sidewalks the guy in the SUV cut right in front of me without looking Celeste and Julia run full tilt into the school yard in the café Bob the anarchist Bob says in the old days we walked to school take Sparky for his wash trim and claw clip at Pet Spa in the old days I washed my dog traffic backed up on Somerville Ave. they'll be digging Somerville and Highland up it'll fuck things up at least through next December kill business there'll be no place to park Molly says anarchism is impossible because too many people have mush for brains Bill on the phone drop off new Pressed Wafer books on his way back from the Cornell show and what about the Jim Behrle Show Sunday morning persistent drizzle leftover lasagna for kids breakfast two tofu breakfast sausage and two eggs with whole wheat toast for me can we have lunch tomorrow or the next day Amanda writes neither can work for me how about later next week that's too far in the future four Flat Nine songs and I could listen to Dave play guitar all day Dear Mary I won't be doing any more substitute teaching Dear Joe we met at Tom O'Grady's party a couple of weeks ago I wonder if you would like to read at our poetry series in East Bridgewater we can't pay you a lot but you will get an attentive audience I remember the party well I met a man who knew "Pickles" Spadafora famed Malden junkyard man I will come to read but I don't know how to get to East Bridgewater Gerrit's raving about a novel called *Savage Detectives* talk of Amanda could she be one of the immortals and the literary conference a panel on Olson my father pronounced Pickles Peekels drizzle to rain Dear Gardeners looks like today will be a washout who stole the egg from the bald eagle steroids did he take them or not there's a war going on and this guy's writing about laundry and breakfast Ginsberg's a faggot a pedophile and the claws of our eagles will rip out your eyes his Red Sox cap and rage hazed eyes I think that was a good poem me too can I recite some Shakespeare today's Sun Ra's birthday I saw him yesterday he sat on a branch one of the grand maples on upper Central Street legs dangling barefoot sequin robe and swami hat he smiled I waved pulled the car over when I got out he was gone like Chih-jen free of all limitations and concepts beyond the limits of this external world Gerrit phones he spent the day with Patrick Barron Eco-Poetics scholar and translator of Zanzotto they walked Dogtown plumber says three-ninety-five to fix both sinks but you should replace your piping and garbage disposal it's bottom of the barrel quality seven hundred for that we'll take the three-ninety-five just fix the leaks bacon and couscous for Julia bacon and scrambled egg Celeste Daddy I don't think we need any jackets any more it's nice and warm and all connected Julia says we're stopped at a red light poetry music and painting it's all connected you have to have music for poetry and painting has images music has sounds and you name them by words people in the front house listen to sports talk radio all day guys argue sports like poets argue poetry it will be two or three years before he lives up to his potential to be a great pitcher how can you say that the other guy says tell me how can you say that there must be poets who need two or three years to live up to their potential Jim Behrle to the left with his microphone Ron Silliman to the right Ron says Jim how do you see tonight's reading shaping up well Ron Jim says as you know you've got a couple of real dickheads reading tonight there's no place in the house I can escape the constant sports banter and beer commercials I'll put my stereo speakers in the window and blast the Ramones day and night see how they like it now it's fly season there's one pissing me off winging around the studio like a World War II fighter it's the third world war he says all over the world we are at war with terrorists borrow pick and shovel from Michael dig trench for water drainage side of the house twenty feet long one foot deep dig up rocks roots plants Christmas tree from years ago vines pull rip swing pick shovel old lost kids' toys temps over ninety you have to stop now Molly says you're overheated and sunburned return today spread liner line with rocks wrap liner over and cover with dirt three more sides of the house need tending don't want to think of how much to do the Tao will complete things to their ends sends mixed messages music painting sight and sound ether couples with itself to create etheric patterns corresponding to the possible past and futures of any moment nothing is more important as anything else roaming the hills deer hunting stunted windblown landscape gnarled tree trunks and branches made of deer antlers suddenly the wind stops a feather drops it is my will to be less angry and hurtful towards those I care for there is no light no absence of light delight in failing change star to star two red dots deer's eyes in headlights I've seen a boy shoot a thousand-pound fifteen-foot-long wild boar with a pistol in Alabama girls painting at the kitchen table Julia acrylics Celeste water colors landscapes trees hills skies clouds greens blues whites rivers oceans this will be just the background stove and dishwasher fixed two-hundred-and-forty Memorial Day Parade was that Mrs. Harris in the Grand Marshall car soldiers navy guys veterans from foreign wars colonial soldiers shooting muskets into the air state police local police mounted police firemen in shiny fire trucks sirens blasting and clans of plaid kilted bagpipers fat men with funny tasseled hats riding tiny cars clowns baton twirlers drummers and buglers the mayor waving to all his supporters while handing out American flags and heard the lady next to me who knew everyone in the parade piercing shouts RACHEL RACHEL RACHEL JOYCE JOYCE JOYCE WHERE'S JOHNNY LOOK THERE'S ANGELA ANGELA ANGELA Rex Trailer's still alive that can't be the original Trigger and the Sons of Italy Marching Band the local garden club an armored truck from the sheriff's department the guy playing the big bass drum is marching in place on horse poop and then more horse poop and more

people and vehicles flatten it motorcycles steer fig-
ure eights down Highland Ave. slush and balloon
venders and flags wave yes Celeste it was the same
parade as last year there was a man he tried to catch
the sun no matter how far he traveled he never got
any closer eventually he died of thirst this is known
as three in the afternoon Celeste you can't wear the
same pants to school every day Celeste don't cry I
only want you to wear clean clothes to school yes
Julia you can have corn on the cob for breakfast no
I cannot chaperone the field trip yes there will be
someone here for the furniture delivery on Friday
the squirrel leaps onto the tree trunk Sparky nar-
rowly missing recently another dead bird on the
sidewalk Sparky shits once down the street and once
on the way back five-forty-five in the morning
Oxford Street silent baked chicken legs with oyster
mushrooms cheesy brown rice and spinach salad
Askold writes that in Beruit bombs exploded within
a mile of his hotel four-fifteen in the morning full
moon orange silver dollar Molly and girls asleep
Sparky asleep birds yet to call three loads of clothes
one load of dishes weed around the patio plant
tomato plants one in each pot workman sings offkey
along to Beatles "Sgt. Peppers" on classic hits station
forty years ago this week weekend anchorwoman
says the greatest rock record of all time photo of
weatherwoman in hospital bed with newly born

baby girl and a cat with fifteen lives more after the break I have spoken out inappropriately so many times an army of tanks couldn't overtake my words sometimes when I read passages that begin with the words people today I'm confused whether it means people this day or two thousand years ago when the words were written how to overcome a lifetime of being accustomed to anger big bee buzz bounces off the screen in the end we flatten out and return to our origin brief thunder showers followed by sunshine through purple-black clouds air conditioner's always on here she says handing me my espresso Dear Friends we will be hosting a Kerouac scroll party on June 21 kids welcome please arrive around noon for burgers fake burgers dogs and beer after which we will go over to view the scroll where's the craft in Kerouac she asks visiting writers always say things like that and write lines like we could have flown to Madagascar they land in Iowa who won the P.J. O'Pootertootle Award for best last line I say to the Master Master I say I have read the ancient books I have tried to put their teachings into practice year in year out no closer to the way than when I started still angry and hurtful I want people to speak highly of me I can't follow things the way they are I want for money success I compete and refuse to admit that things must end showing my strengths to cover up my weaknesses there's no happiness nor sorrow

I can understand buried in illusions how connect body and mind the poem imprisoned by social convention and useless worries awake at night thinking the difference between right and wrong front or back left or right anger emerges from non-anger flying birds return to their homelands I am too proud full of myself forceful provocative fond of forming grudges my mind is not orderly my troubles exist before a word is written I can only dream of being virtuous unable to resign myself to what cannot be avoided I cannot accept hardship wearing out my brain trying to make many things into one what am I to do Master I say the Master says nothing he stands silent for nearly a week then gouges my eyes two-inch downpour new water trench works perfectly Diamante Poems For Celeste kind fun playing running jumping gold mouse Disneyworld Charlotte's Web coloring drawing writing nice funny kind friendly running playing smiling girl sister book squat tag coloring painting helping funny friend happy fast kicking painting running soccer field center wing saving screaming shopping helpful playful cool funny running helping reading school home girl classmate writing talking walking friendly clever blue gold stomping running jumping dog dad sister mom writing drawing laughing kind nice nice kind playing jumping reading mom dad Anna Ruby running swimming bouncing blue red nice smart jumping playing walking soccer girl sister kid reading writing talking good great gold blue running jumping tagging girl friend classmate daughter reading writing drawing nice kind seven eight jumping running reading Anna Ruby Claire good times drawing walking writing nice funny funny nice running drawing writing dolls dog student girl caring helping playing cool pretty funny kind running playing jumping soccer ball art school laughing reading writing blue fast active thoughtful helping jumping passing balls China dad work thinking playing measuring fun observant nice playing drawing reading books catch math animals jumping running walking kind person nice kind playing jumping running Ruby Calvin Claire Anna acting singing dancing funny awesome nice girls helping running jumping park Anna toy movies eating sleeping walking kind fun fast short running jumping laughing mom dad sister girl joking playing talking kind friendly fun good singing dancing writing mom dad school home loving sharing caring cool nice friendly funny riding biking dangling home school mom dad reading writing running loud helpful kind pretty running playing jumping books pens China dolls walking eating talking stylish run fast excellent likes pizza sweet happy drawing thinking trying ideas paper pencils colors helping writing learning poetic exotic the body of the missing American soldier found floating

in the river we'll talk with his grief-stricken parents
roses burst on our lone shabby bush yes I will work
the lights for the grades five through eight annual
talent show today Celeste readies for her Kung Fu
orange belt test Julia critiques her in tighten your
elbow get down lower in Horse Position turn your
left foot when you kick with your right slow down
pay attention to the details all I got was my eyes
gouged it goes to show there is no life and no death
and I a fool trying to catch the sun can't be Donne
been dead a long time Molly phones says the head
doctor falls asleep during morning meetings last
night a patient walked off the unit and nobody
noticed grass trees and plants spring to life early
tomato Bunker Hill Monument shrouded in grey fog
bones discovered in tunnels under a local historic
cemetery two loads towels two bed linens breaded
chicken baked potatoes and salad every time they
walk in my trench to retrieve their soccer ball they
kick in debris that will soot up the trench she's
found wandering confused second time in a week I
wasn't lost I knew where I was going I was going to
the donut shop to meet the girls I've been walking
there for years you can't lock me in here I'll move
and get my own place we strive for certain things
certain those things make us happy I'm not happy
with it but I'm trying not to be unhappy sometimes
when I say in ancient times I don't mean another

millennium but forty years ago when I was a boy before I met Chang Kuo-lao and the notion of time became essential in relation to primordial chaos it's eight-thirty take a bike ride play soccer but first you have to clean the living room it's a mess and it's all your stuff drive to South Medford buy ravioli from the widow at Bella stop at pharmacy cold remedy for Julia Dear Bill how's tricks in Vermont Dear Mr. Torra it is time to have your blood levels checked Dear Joe thanks for the Wieners book I have been reading it aloud during my overnight shift at the guard desk something about the written word spoken aloud I especially like "Poem for Painters" she's been accused of reconstructing the people she's lost and how it's all patch work I was born in China I was with my dad I was so excited when I was with him I went on a plane with him to go to America when I left the plane I saw my sister Julia and my mom it was my first time seeing my sister then it was my mom's first time seeing me she was happy I was happy very happy I like to play with my cousins and aunts and uncles and I like to take bubble baths when I was four we got our dog his name is Sparky I like to take care of Sparky when I got my first doll house it was important to me he was last seen riding the two roads with one donkey fly flew in when I opened the door I don't think you should kill Tommy off at the end of the story Somerville Ave.

closed this morning traffic heavy on Highland to from Davis Square to the McGrath and O'Brien twenty minutes down the block she doesn't want to go to the dances she can't remember the steps gets frustrated and sits down and she's messing up the Bingo cards at the Soldier's Home Gerrit points to the house he and Derek rented in the 1960s for sixty dollars a month female turkey along mosquito infested Old Rockport Road brilliantly colored cock pheasant no mushrooms but large hawk eating a gray squirrel allows us to get within yards people behind us party two and three nights a week until two and three in the morning music and voices escalate as the night progresses smell grilling meat Julia and I bike path to Davis Square to Albion Street all the way to Central cross Highland turn left on Oxford hello to Cathy on the corner Peg stops us come in and see my new mosaics soccer in the street with Celeste car coming run up on sidewalk Dad you need to practice at aiming waves smash against the seawall storm's been circling off the coast for two days spray up over the wall onto the walk we should have brought umbrellas she says it's cold we walk against the wind gray purple icy-green there used to be a lot of older guys who came down here to walk but now they're all gone and Aunt Gloria phoned and wants me to go there in August how the girls doing Joe I watch the television but today I didn't I sometimes will but to tell you the truth so I didn't I well sometimes I only watch it I don't even maybe at night I sit and there's where she got chased by the dog one time with my sister best not intervene with the course of things let them unfold according to their own nature rear town-house tier rare sayeth the preacher bottom of stairs area clean organize trash unused broken items vacuum with power vac pick up girls last day of school have a nice summer you too have a nice summer too have a nice summer you too Amanda hasn't written so I'll imagine she wrote that some days she doesn't really believe any of it not one bit but mostly she accepts the way things unfold she saw Mike's band at PA's she danced and felt sexy guys watched her and thought she was hot did I show you the picture of my mother she looks so what's the word they use battered yes battered no never oh no never he never hit her he put her in the hospital oh that was when he drank when they had sex first day of vacation and donuts for breakfast I am a mediocre man never traveled the Dark Obscurity nor returned to the Great Thoroughfare they say a sacred basset hound lives in the neighborhood Sparky and I set out to find the beast after seventeen days returned home unsuccessful Julia naps Sparky naps Celeste on the computer Molly working at the hospital one load in the washer one in the dryer follow the bike trail down to Davis to Mass. Ave. cross over into Cambridge onto Alewife Station didn't take us long Dad straight lines usually won't ambulance in front of the neighbors house old lady wrapped up to just below the chin on the stretcher one of her daughters by her side in the poem Li Po meets Tu Fu after a long absence and one of them asks if the other got eaten by poetry peonies have come and gone roses hanging on tomatoes coming strong in the pots over to check the garden raspberries nearly ready tomatoes slow lettuce soon hawk on top of an old oak tree rub the Buddha's belly you say the battle not the war ongoing battle it is war ongoing who going on to the next round won today the next poet I see I will ask hey what happened did the poem eat you let's get the show on the road Celeste says rides off on her new blue bike with training wheels round and round the schoolyard Father's Day Iggy and the Stooges live at the Whiskey A Go-Go poster thought you'd like it Molly says she cooks ribs potato salad tomato and cucumber salad cold beers Dear Joe sorry to be out of touch for so long and sorry I never got back to you about the literary agent I was sued by one of my ghost writer clients for three million dollars and I've been putting everything I've got into that hopefully it will be over soon you can imagine how all-consuming it has been I don't know what we're going to do about the traffic paint a tree on an old landscape I'm a writer who paints others are poets who paint others are both painters and poets and need not the sub-appellation a this who does that some are painters who play music others are musicians who paint then there are the real painters and musicians and car racers also plumbers who can what clan they don't even come out of the same door at school there are more forms of the Great Clod along the Great Thoroughfare only to morph into morning I wander in Somerville old shopping carriage on its side edge of the bike trail smell goods baking at Lindell's stop for a slush with the girls sit on the side of the schoolyard with Celeste riding her bike having imaginary conversation with myself Amanda writes that she's tired from the heat and it isn't yet summer baby crying upstairs dolls on the washing machine her mother's MRI find a box fold a blanket clean spiders off new bookcase try to find things she doesn't need "When I Go Deaf" when she goes deaf I'm sorry I lost my patience and yelled it's okay Dad no it isn't because I always say I'm sorry and then do it again this is called saying you are sorry and doing it again shrieks of Julia and Celeste playing outside eight green tomatoes rose bushes heavy droop stay in or stay out and don't slam the door air conditioner creates white noise so the birds don't wake me at dawn sleep until six cereal Celeste Julia Italian wedding soup slice of pizza me one slice

toasted dark rye butter and peach jam coffee salute
the rising sun sing all day under blue or gray skies
this is known as singing all day under blue or gray
skies do not practice singing all day under blue and
gray skies if you practice allowing the semen to
return because there's a risk of penis root decay Dear
Joe it seems like small press has served you well I'd
like to talk with you some time and learn more
about how it all works when I first started out I
thought that's where I was headed did I ever tell you
how I ended up publishing with a big house and
writing for the glossies Julia flings the ball right into
the gutter time after time but Celeste takes the ball
in both hands rolls it from between her legs knocks
those candlepins down I throw two or three gutter
balls then a strike bowling's big balls to some people
little balls to others I grew up playing with both big
balls and little balls have no preference Sacco Lanes
in Davis Square 1950s not a thing changed half
decade where my childhood chum's older brother
got taken by a pool shark La Contessa Bakery closes
last of old Davis Square except for Dente's barber
shop no more rum cakes cannoli Italian cookies
whipped cream cakes lobster tails apple turnovers
lemon turnovers strawberry turnovers brownies
apple pies Boston cream pies oversize muffins bis-
cotti Neapolitans coffee espresso although the
machine was rarely working special Easter cream

cheese pies waffle cookies chocolate éclairs cheese-cake chocolate cake vanilla cake chocolate frosting chocolate cookies M & M cookies oatmeal raisin cookies Danish cinnamon buns opening soon a sushi bar and rumor is McIntyre and Moore Books is on the way out on Saturday night the dykes line up to get into Toast in Union Square where you can hear music at PA's or the The Nog or Sally O'Brien's cheap Indian Thai burgers Chinese Mexican Western Union best place to cash checks in quotes Brazil Bakery Brazil Insurance Hispanic market Indian market Asian market and Elegant Furniture old painted white sign with red and green letters faded peeled destined for postcard photograph enjoy it while you can he says it's the next square in the city to scale up one size fits all but on the box it says extra large Ed Barrett's *Kevin White* in the reflection of the Hancock Tower's pornographic glass skin the pumpkin clay roof of Trinity Church for its Hajj across Boston's postage stamp size Celtic fields where St. Catherine sits in a tree eating cherries with Fanny Howe oh no Fanny Howe is allergic to cherries I heard it from a monk who makes machine gun noises through his mouth decisions go the wrong way because the skill was never there to begin with this is called some decisions go the wrong way because the skill was never there to begin with I like to be there when the day starts and when it stops

Stephen Jonas knows what's buried under the Trinity Church but people won't listen because he hears voices in his teeth o Davis Square Starbucks crêpes sushi and Northern Italian how do we assess what the city planners do with many millions budgets what had they better do snake run over by car middle of Oxford Street upper half squished and lifeless rear half writhing that's a terrible thing to have to see Dad Amanda writes that as she writes Sam is standing up straight so the girls had a half day no they're on vacation oh they're on vacation the tidal river divides the two towns Julia and Celeste explore tidal pools it's a life extravaganza Julia says snails little fish crabs and mussels used to see a lot of guys walking here but they're all gone now and there's where the dog chased us so the girls had a half day today no they're on vacation oh they're on vacation white sails far out on the harbor moms with kids blankets baskets shovels pails hats sun screen chairs water toys tuna salad or peanut butter and jelly Chinese Julia says dumplings vegetables noodles shrimp spring rolls soup they eat good God bless them Marina called and she wants to come up for a day I think she said Saturday with this friend I don't think I met I may have met her once Marina says I met her before but I can't remember what does your fortune say who cares about the Kerouac scroll it's just a piece of crap Gavin says thirty feet of one the hundred-twenty rolled out under glass please do not lean no photographs but Jim uses his cell phone camera bebop piped in Kerouac 101 type displays on the wall not stopping to break the narrative rhythm by having to put a fresh piece of paper in the typewriter dense single spaced long meandering sentences Gerrit once owned a Cornell bought it for three hundred later when he was broke sold it for six hundred and now it's worth a hundred thousand and he met Kerouac at John LaTouche's place Ryan cooks hot dogs burgers fish cakes sausages Amanda's pasta salad beer Ryan's paintings and collages hang high and low Buddhas poets Shakespeare next to Derek's deer antlers faces of the men and the women exaggerated features blues reds toddlers tug of wars over baby carriages and balls Jim riding the swing chanting some crazy chant Gerrit wears cool shades Mike's new tattoo he's cutting some wires on my car engine what are you doing to my car he speaks back an unknown foreign language this is my car but he continues to cut more wires threaten to phone the cops but he doesn't stop I call the cops they send a young detective in a trench coat short and moustache who can't speak the same language that the man speaks Amanda writes that greens are fresh from the garden coffee is hot cream sweet sunrise with birds a-twit babies crying baking a cake with almonds butter lemon don't open the mail what is it she is looking for and who can say so little to do when the sky keeps falling blue for hours killing the green bug lands on her chest don't touch the sides don't connect don't hit a wall as if the little plastic femur fills in empty parts of us when they don't know what to do with themselves pin the tail on the donkey or Operation put the pieces in rain hide away O poet of Gloucester knower of sacred locations Ed Barrett says we came here in a time machine somebody else invented wherever you are it is the real world red brick-faced house wrought iron railings small box windows with statues of the Virgin Mary Saint Anthony Saint Francis and Jesus himself in the inverted tub on the front lawn rows of tomatoes down the side of the house I see the old bald man shirtless and all too fleshy in shorts that look like boxers black socks and sandals tending to his kingdom I don't think I ever told Ed that my cousin found human bones along Route 93 while looking for shed deer antlers he reported it to the police they said they'd take care of it later he went to the same area found more human bones walked back to the spot where he first saw the other bones and they were still there brought one to the police station placed it on the desk and said there's bones out there and soon detectives took my cousin in a room putting pressure how did he know the bones were there my cousin told them he was looking for

antlers it's a hobby and while deer hunting in the
fall he sits in a tree rubs antlers together so a buck
will come looking for a fight and when the buck gets
close enough he shoots it it's said a lot of the bodies
were dumped right along 93 new collage I will name
"Organs of want beyond bounds" air is hot breeze
relieves man whistling imitations of bird calls Dear
Joe I am applying for a residency at Yaddo and I was
wondering if you might consider writing a letter I
realize this is probably a bad time and you are trying
to enjoy your summer clean basement dead mice
broken fluorescent light bulbs rotted carpet useless
books broken baby carriage worn baby backpack
out to trash move boxes of books one side to the
other barbell and weights to corner find old paint-
ings one "Self-Portrait" stored upside down mouse
piss rots the top part of my head eats the paint off
chicken wings rice and spinach there a moment
when summer hangs forever in breath-long lull
water weed bean patch put down mulch tomatoes
strong tarragon parsley oregano bay leaf sage ready
pick sweet lettuce toss with fresh herbs vinegar oil
dash of honey mustard sauté broccoli with olive oil
and garlic pinch of salt and pepper Swiss chard ready
peppers showing nicely lots more weeding watering
essential in the heat peas should be picked next
week Taylor says and I won't be here don't let things
go to waste this is known as not reaping the harvest

I just wanted to have babies he seemed like a nice
guy quiet in the beginning I didn't like his mother
but he seemed like a nice Italian boy and I don't
remember Marina's friend she knew her a long time
they were friends when Marina was young but
Marina says the lady she remembers she's older
than Marina and fat and the girls they'll be out
of school or they're still in school oh they're out of
school another mother unloads her wagon bag after
bag of all the gear a mother must pack to take two
kids to the beach chilly today for the beach remem-
ber when we used to go to Revere Beach when you
were small I don't know this area but I think maybe
we should have gone the other way Ma you told me
this way well when I'm not driving myself I get con-
fused leap into the boundless and make it your
home fly high burrow deep dog shit everywhere
why don't owners pick it up Sparky squats for his
second interrupted by cat perched on a porch rail
lunges at the fleeing cat hold him back with leash
smell incense from Peg's yard she mediates on her
deck SUV starts up by remote startles swimming in
the air above the tree tops and roofs the doctor
wrote awake early to the white blare of a sun flood-
ing in sidewise strip and bathe in it you walk bare-
foot in Somerville she asks she'll meet him you know
where on the dark side it's always in fashion to talk
about the moon what is the name of this month's

moon Julia says baiting a hook is one of life's great pleasures and these are some fat crawlers wind slaps waves against the dock whitecaps on lake kids catch bluegills small bass fat sunfish yellow perch beer batter fish potatoes onion rings and artichoke hearts Sauvignon Blanc wind settles lake still remove shorts slip behind dock swim out from dock water clear and cool slow breast stroke stop doggy paddle elementary back stroke roll over breast stroke pontoon boat full of people straight my way swim hard for dock just in time sneak behind a boat as they pontoon by chicken mushrooms side of old stump too old to eat dried and rubbery color turning from the bright orange to bronze those would have been good a week ago Dad the wind picks up through morning kids play with shovels bury treasures bones stones charms traps and plots chipmunks moles mice ants bees lone fisherman quietly fishing his way down around docks and moored boats where a monster lurks and the speedboats with hundred plus inboards and jet skis canoes sailboats rowboats bass boats kayaks pontoon boats water skiers fireworks light up the lake late night the pops and booms hang for silent moments after the burst before reaching us cheers echo across the water more whistles bangs and bright choreographed explosions to celebrate this day Jim calls he's at work and he kind of wishes he wasn't it sucks but what can you do when your world is ruled he calls them improvisations looking at the other side of the door or both edges on a blade of grass and leaves fall more by the buds that push them off than by lack of greenness he must know he's a doctor books pile around me guitars cases amp paintings against the wall stacked on the floor paints brushes easel guitar straps and cords boxes of Pressed Wafer books on top of the other boxes of correspondence makeshift shelf overflowing with teaching-related records student portfolios mass of reading handouts large fan blowing anything light and loose around on its journey side to side folded chairs fishing rods tackle box nowhere to move but small path from the door to the chair at this desk I could be doing right now something productive the old lady still lives wrapped in a blanket on this the Fourth of July she looks right through me and she looks scared Amanda writes about a certain feeling floating in water at moonlight trying to make up with poetry and love poems fresh peas with ginger the car makes a grinding noise when the brake is applied have it towed someone sweeps her rug cleans folds dumps out her pocketbook fills it with Legos I had more friends ten years ago but I've pissed a few people off over the years already been a week my mother the girls and I walk the beach Chinese food Joe can you buy beer and keep it in your house of course well where would

you keep it in the refrigerator oh in the refrigerator
there is beginning and not yet beginning electrician
in the café and the café woman got a thing going
how much effort spent looking for clarity instead of
seeing clearly summer insects thrive pick lettuce
chard broccoli raspberries juicy sweet eat them all
walking home Spanish music from the open win-
dows along Highland good to have food you've
started from seed Julia asks you ate all those rasp-
berries Somerville Ave. closed from Central to Cedar
down Park towards Cambridge left on Beacon loop
back catch Somerville Ave. in Union Square up Mon-
ument left onto Highland thick traffic ten minutes
down to School right on Oxford this is known as
closing a section of one road fucking up traffic in the
rest of the city Confucius said don't to go in and
hide don't come out and shine stand still in the mid-
dle he must be wise he quoted Confucius but who
the fuck wants to stand still in the middle what do
you do when you get there stop run upstairs get cof-
fee back again begin again John Wieners' *A Book of
Prophecies* inferno purgatory heavenly John who as
child spied Fanny Howe hiding under his front
porch until the police came yes that's what you went
to Harvard for would you rather end up rust proof-
ing cars in a Kia dealership not that there's anything
wrong with that I rust proofed cars at an Oldsmobile
dealership but it's not for someone gifted as your

boy Bob calls he's meeting a committee about rais-
ing a statue in Worcester Sacco and Vanzetti he'll
give a talk and slide show self-proclaimed anarchist
doing a presentation to erect a statue in Worcester o
Errico Malatesta visit my dreams we'll take Medford
and Malden then forge the Mystic River take
Somerville Cambridge then broaden our campaign
and liberate Charlestown we could even raise some
hell in Boston with a pointed guerilla effort it's all a
matter of educating people if we can get to people
we'll dig up the bodies along Route 93 expose the
entire enterprise for what it is people will finally see
and then and then Neil says people are stupid he
always says people are stupid we have a second
espresso a real estate agent shows the condos in the
house directly behind us a middle-aged couple look-
ing better suited for suburbs conversations of new
kitchens floors walls ceilings windows roof porches
central air freshly painted white fences views of
Boston skyline desirable property indeed Celeste
comes down stairs gives me a hug says I just wanted
to come down and give you a hug what has no form
what has no change I've waited all night by the
street light then the moon grows fat in the sky we
set up tents cook on fire wild cats appear in the night
leave the gear climb in the car drive away fast until
first light my father says I didn't know they got the
dog they must have torn it up he plays with the

snake if it bites you die within two minutes he says
the snake nearly slithers out of the boy's hands but
he grabs it just in time and it continues you think
the snake is getting away the boy gets control maybe
it's part of the show wash dry and fold put their own
clothes away Sunday morning at eight workmen
return to finish various jobs around the new condos
shouting banging sawing when you go to sleep on
your belly you dream of snakes so no more belly
sleeping Latinos play soccer in Dilboy Field Julia
gives Celeste swimming lessons paddle with your
legs now harder blue and gold red and white uni-
forms figures running up and down the field men's
voices carrying across the park Spanish tongues
water's cold turns Celeste's skin red Julia dreams
Molly dyes her hair blond but it comes out white
notebook entry nearly two years ago to this day The
Cosmos in the center of the wheel TAO the center is
the light where lives the color black sitting here
study chair girls upstairs master of my there Amanda
writes cheese curls what are we coming to large
glass jar full of plastic beads smell coffee and ciga-
rettes she winds yarn from a cone made of silk and
wool the color of grass tired of the burden of prod-
uct she doesn't pray but knits memories in each
stitch trying not to get any memories wrong egg rolls
with homemade duck sauce plums and apples
swimming in waves after hurricanes legs raw from

barnacles on the rocks sort laundry clean living room kitchen needs thorough cleaning starting with the stove cabinets appliances brown chicken legs sauté garlic in olive oil add tomatoes salt pepper fresh basil oregano parsley and simmer high for about half an hour then add the browned chicken legs cook over a low heat for an hour serve over noodles and a side of pan-seared greens what about the gutter and they still need to finish whatever more realtors more curious couples I can see the tops of their heads hear every word from where I sit the birds happy don't give a hop who lives where as a rule people don't like prose poems in the interview I'm wearing a black turtle neck sweater they haven't had a party at the house behind us since the cops showed up one night sent them inside no more Latino sounds my neighbor shows me his score card from shooting his bow fine tuning for the deer season if I get meat you get meat essence equals spirit spirit equals being being equals doing you can be several places at the same time energy assembles becomes essence this is no coincidence a woman's strength can tame a lion he who carries his own lamp walks in the universe amidst the stars what is the difference between one extra spot light radiates in ripples around Julia and Celeste's wisdom justice is measured by the fangs of the measurer hanged by one's own hands I must tone down my dominant

behavior I stepped outside my culture society rela-
tionships personality beliefs prejudices opinions
ideas and it scared the shit out of me I have no mid-
dle ground I do as I will on illusory plane nothing
important as anything I saw The Venerable Lord he
looks like the last time I saw him death earth mind
future dark present chaos light heaven time body
form fire sun moon did he really write love in the
middle of all that too all your towers no matter how
well erected will collapse and crumble don't say I
don't care about the war because I don't write about
it or sign petitions how quick stick dreams I chase
everywhere in the old cabin rushing rivers trails
high ridges forest fishy streams deer leap from
grassy beds the water the water the woods the
woods the woods' roads and squishy old leather
boot creaky wooden floor hardware store or diner
ham and egg sandwich where I wake from sleep dif-
ference between one and the other is Tao swim fish
canoe the kids Julia and Avery catch frogs Melissa
catches a pickerel hike to the Pinnacle forty-five
minutes to the top view the surrounding valleys dis-
tant dairy farms rivers and ponds Mark says his
favorite part of the hike is when the trail turns into
mud Julia dizzy overheated late afternoon sun Avery
climbs the fireplace chimney can't get down Bob the
drummer Bob and Mary Jo serves fresh anchovies
olives local cheeses cream butter berries pasta with

mushrooms broccoli and cream sauce white wine on the road back to the city near midnight listen to Willie DeVille MC5 Jonathan Richman Nick Lowe asleep in the back dream of frogs swimming mountains fresh-picked strawberries with local heavy cream sprinkled with maple sugar Gerrit phones meet him and Ken in Davis Square the Tibetan restaurant Ken on annual visit from Kansas every July Mike phones can't talk eating with Ken and Gerrit Mike says tell Gerrit he got his message and called back and left him a message people I once laughed at have made fortunes a few won poetry prizes things occur in perfectly prepared stages power can be restored with reserves in place carry this effect to its target those which act as a basis to receive impressions or an anchor can be non-local instantaneously available everywhere each time I quit coffee for tea I return to coffee dead rodent on the sidewalk baby bat or mouse must do this must do that oppression is enemy of creation seclusion and visualizing led me to Oh Tep Min and the enormity of the whole of intangible time to a thin stream we call real time instead of a three-dimensional temporal continuum through time and practice the body becomes more of a cosmic entity in Julia's dream she's engulfed by a giant banana I witness a murder but nobody believes me at the poetry reading I jump up to the podium why would I make something like this up but nobody will listen not even Bill who prints money on an old-fashioned press turns out sheets of tens and twenties the pregnant Chinese woman says people only adopt because they can't have one of their own wash Sparky on patio with the garden hose hold him tight lather up rinse let go he shakes rolls more shakes cut and clear all the brush and weeds back of the house fill two yard waste bags bike down the bike path through Davis across to Mass. Ave. ride the sidewalk to Arlington with Julia stop for snack and water bike back a different route bike around the block with Celeste her training wheels stop talk with Peg maybe a block party in August drive to Medford cheese ravioli at Bella the mom says in Italy nobody had nothing and everyone was happy long as you had a dish of pasta her son who weighed two hundred sixty weighs two hundred stopped drinking twelve cokes a day and rides his bike Celeste cereal Julia leftover breaded chicken me half bagel cream cheese and jam three cups coffee squirrel leaps from pine bough to roof of neighbor's garage runs along the gutter stops stares at me skips away more raspberries today summer's first tomato cut it up toss with freshly picked lettuce splash of oil and vinegar pinch salt and pepper vacuum corner cobwebs in kitchen take down art work notices calendar summer Kung Fu schedule last year's class list photos of

the girls last old Christmas cards wash walls floor-
boards cabinets stove refrigerator dishwasher win-
dow sills window and door frames warm drizzly July
afternoon Molly phones from work just checking in
everybody's been to the Cornell show but me Ger-
rit's seen it five times oh you must go you must go
to the Cornell show more dreams rivers woods and
camps bird of prey eating flesh morning Sun Saluta-
tions and the nine Asanas first time in over a year
since shoulder injury body older stiffer fatter bones
and joints buckle and crack cup of coffee make
Molly's lunch take out trash walk Sparky get break-
fast ready for girls Ken backs over a rock garden wall
in Gerrit's yard they need a tow truck to get the car
out at dawn the soldiers leave the safety of their out-
posts and ride a thousand miles into their fate he
said that's part of our strategy they're leaving the
safety of their outposts and riding to their fate you
said you read her baby's coughing she has a doctor
appointment this afternoon there's peas to pick flow-
ers too make a list things to do check email reply to
friends tell stories to birds stories that make beaks
grow to bite cherries young blonde couple early thir-
ties tan shorts green shirts carry boxes up stairs to
the second floor of the condo cut bags of herbs dry
on the window sills smell thyme tarragon oregano
sage three more tomatoes kale and lettuce chard
weed and mulch Taylor and Julia plant second crop

lettuce Celeste waters Paul carries weed piles down to the compost heap pick pint of raspberries collards chard marinade chicken in fresh herbs garlic and lemon roast serve with sauté of garden greens tossed with pasta I gave a reading in East Bridgewater and nobody came I didn't give the reading it was canceled because no one came first time that no one came once I gave a reading and two people came in ancient times this is known as two people coming to your reading Dorchester gas tanks Boston skyline lit up Saturday night traffic fast tracking cars race past both sides of me doing the speed limit now it's out about the Virgin Mary chipped blue and white paint surrounded by donkeys owls elves fairies ducks frogs angels flamingos plastic flowers ribbons the little fountain spills into a little pond front of the house new shrink asks am I still writing I ask is he still shrinking it's so still outside Sunday afternoon summer my desk and computer overrun with red ants stroll down the street with Sparky on leash she doesn't want to go to the senior citizen's center because it's full of old people she doesn't need the van it's close enough that she can walk photo from Olson conference Gloucester what year Barbara Blatner Bob D'Attilio Molly T.J. Anderson Chris Patricia Michael Nick Lawrence Ange Patrick old photo of my uncle Victor in a tuxedo next to my mother on her wedding day North End put out ant killer but killing ants puts you at sixes and sevens with the Way Celeste interrupts looking for her boogie board for the beach tomorrow lose my thread of thought how begin to take delights into old age this and that gave birth but it died Gerrit doesn't like museums he thinks everything is turning museum turning museum that's how he said it the girls ride waves on boogie boards Revere Beach dig in sand cover themselves in mud race into waves walk in to my waist take a leak look around at others out here waist deep probably pissing too Julia and Celeste near brown me white fleshy hairy the well-formed shiny bodies parade up and down the shore Bianchi's pizza with soda under the boulevard pigeons gather in the eaves this is good pizza Julia says but you need to eat it right out of the oven if it cools too much you lose the crust traffic backed up along the Revere Beach Parkway snake our way home Molly phones she's getting out of work an hour early see you soon man whacks weeds in the yard of the new condo artificial hands arms legs feet he never thought he could skate again at night they patrol the perimeters using the most advanced technology doing nothing is a movement in ancient times but doing nothing isn't necessarily not doing something this is known as doing nothing isn't necessarily not doing something we have a catalogue full of sages thousands pages Chou proverb says you can kill a peasant by

letting him sit down what is there to study anyhow
I live by the manners I was taught they weren't the
best this is known as fate then passing unhindered
through solid objects or ride the empty air after this
book I will devote all my skills to something new I
know not yet what fish hike camp skate bowl dance
act learn a trade music paint cook open a business
work with animals become a horse person bird twirp
twirp twirp silence then twirp twirp twirp then old
photo Aunt Rose oldest of my mother's sisters dance
outfit age fifteen 1930 next thing you know they
take out a photo album and you're in for a second
cup of coffee dung beetles roll balls of dung you
dream and know you are dreaming act rest and
change it says human life requires spirit and energy
there's diet restrictions alone would kill me but fly-
ing around on the back of a great bird for all eternity
low lying small plane out the window ninety degrees
that looks like a Jackson Pollock the blonde anchor-
woman says about the painting done by the chimp
news from Red Sox Nation next o star in a puddle of
flowery style to hide your true intentions I examine
myself with great care Jim not the other Jim but Jim
Behrle writes a television audition another year's
worth of things to do I like the sauce she says pours
my cup of tea over her rice no walk today too hot sit
in shade look out over Swampscott Harbor stories
from her past in starts and stops oh I can't remember

don't get old how are the girls doing and Molly tell
her I miss her what is global warming they say
there's too many people and they keep letting them
in and they start driving Ma it's the whole planet not
just our country but they come here and get cars I
am another ignorant one traveling in circles tasting
food before I eat it where go rushing this way and
that the figure points to a knobby hill hot Saturday
morning Julia and I bike down to Union Square
Charlie the barber from Charlestown been in Union
Square forty years quick buzz cut off to the market
pedal home sweating up School Street good to be
inside air conditioning I keep wondering what I
might want to re-invent self be relieved of this curse
my right eye still might be the moon and my left the
sun realizing the one means uncovering human
bones weathered spread out over time by animals
no one will admit anyone can put on a robe and
wear a scarlet belt in ancient times they were known
as robe and belt people revered and sacred you
stride on something and float away oh that's what
they say especially during times of war Jim calls it
Thunder of Fucking and Horns we bike around the
block then slush at the corner store tonight fried
chicken couscous and spinach salad tell someone
around here I don't care the Red Sox great year like
saying I'm an atheist they make death threats over
an interracial couple some quarterback raises pit

bulls for to-the-death fighting I'm afraid what might happen of I miss the local morning news what's Paula wearing today and Scott's patch of gray hair I need to know everything is absurd as I think the kids run up and down the stairs Molly on her computer dishwasher broke doing them by hand red ants continue to swarm the desk sit on the sofa stare at the wall black weight descends hangs and won't let go knots my stomach yoga walk the dog post office with Celeste and Julia espresso at the café girls eat gelato thunderstorms occasional sun breaks Sparky barks at thunder cracks most people do this most people do that take out luggage sort clothes ready for NYC trip tomorrow five days in the city first time for the girls Celeste and Julia already packed Molly sorts through her wardrobe selects outfits weather remains hot and humid twenty-five years ago tomorrow Molly and I rose from our basement apartment in Cambridge and went downtown to get married someone should open up a celestial chariot dealership I'd like to know how to rest for a moment some day I'm going to read all the checked and underlined highlighted exclamation pointed sections of the books in my library book by read only what I've marked he got the head of Goliath confused with the head of John the Baptist which turned out to be the head that Aphrodite was missing it's not a well crafted story and it hasn't reached its potential imagine you are on a beach and you find something o calamity o fortune I think five pairs underwear five pairs socks should be enough t-shirts dress shirts sneakers dress shoes belt shorts jeans dress slacks I know a man shuts the door entertains a blank mind another great show last night the Fringe every Monday at Lily's two hours no sheet music no breaks just flat out to audience of fifteen bigger than poetry Bob says I wonder did the Fringe ever play and nobody came shed and shed until there are nothing but sheds around Eighth Ave. quiet sunny Sunday morning not even a horn beep Celeste says she'd like to live in Manhattan because there's a Nintendo World here Central Park hazy hot walk Battery Park tourists lined up by the thousands for ferries to Ellis Island street performers Julia and Celeste cool off in the sprinklers Museum of Natural History bright frogs poisonous frogs dinosaur movie packs of local summer day camp kids swarm the exhibits whole fish at Greek restaurant rabbit at Italian restaurant dim sum in Chinatown breakfast Olympic Diner mobs in Times Square MOMA Richard Serra Pollock Gorky Guston Miró Cézanne Picasso Klint Kline Motherwell David Smith Giacometti Kokoschka Van Gogh Times Square Toys"R"Us Celeste chooses presents for her eighth birthday hookers hustlers the cabbie who won't take us the cabbies who do take us the lady who tells me she didn't think there'd be good food here and thought she'd have to eat at Applebee's dancers singers doesn't New York have to sleep some time Celeste wants to know women in sexy dresses cleavage cleavage everywhere I sit here looking down from the second floor hotel window in a public bathroom suddenly a sack is placed over my head and I'm dragged away Celeste calls from a wooded area we hear her but can't find her then the woman who flirts with me hits me over the head with a beer bottle when I refuse her advances sit up in the bed blinking neon outside the window Celeste talks in her sleep it just landed there it just landed there o city Amanda writes Sam took four steps killing flies that take over the kitchen satin ribbon rickrack embroidering floss rayon binding zippers untangling ends jingle bells piecing together the story black and green dots a white dove and an olive branch glittering gold tights raw silk scraps rusts and browns cut and iron bake scones for neighbors saving bottle caps and pull tabs Sunday morning sun rise like a pink ghost makes characters to suit needs that gather quiet exuberance and build a life to write middles where nothing was before make stories out of hellos and goodbyes time is an illusion Julia says years months days seconds decades are all lies she cries I'm so confused I'm so confused I want my life the way it used too be I need things but I don't know

what they are why can't I have my car Ed writes wet
cold weather in Ireland this summer two down com-
forters and flannel pajamas high stool days you
want to sit in the pub all day good to be in a
place where no one gives a shit who you are
fisherman untangle their nets strip naked to jump in
the sea for quick washing flesh pink and shivering
undressing and dressing with their front to the
wall because we all have the same bare ass broiled
chicken fresh-picked basil and tomatoes fresh
mozzarella splash olive oil and balsamic vinegar
Sparky diarrhea shits all over the living room floor
down into the heating grate feed him boiled ground
beef mixed with white rice does the trick basement
studio too hot write at kitchen table dishwasher
hum sandalwood fumes yoga and Chinese bells
never put anything in writing the master wrote
moths fly into lamps throw themselves into fire and
die for want of light when you touch a pattern to
fabric you pin it right you master your own life
would if I could control my stubborn mind Gerrit
phones his guests gone he's alone come to visit look-
ing for fish in a tree is futile time has the power to
clap its lid on language if I don't remind the girls to
brush their teeth they won't this is called making
sure your kids brush their teeth any plans for today
Dad who knows how long a house will last knows a
dragon can be large or small what I realize is there

is a foundation of consciousness enters water with-
out drowning fire without burning give up half way
along and you waste your effort when I talk to my
selflessness no one can compete with my expressive-
ness it's one minute past eleven in the morning the
washing machine shifts into spin cycle polka dots
and moonbeams did a drawing that looked more
like patterns speeding past light deadheading the
hydrangea it's a matter of planting good or planting
evil showers stop sun perks up pick raspberries sing
a special song but feel like a traitor when a house
does take over all the stories are sad or about love
and unzippered gingermen they found her body at
the bottom of a ravine the police show up at the
campsite arrest us all the evidence points towards
me in the café Derek complains about Naropa I com-
plain about UMass institution is institution classes
begin in three weeks bike path to Davis Square to
Somerville Ave. down to left on School up the hill
that's the quickest we made it ever Julia says sauté
garlic in olive oil add fresh crushed tomatoes basil
and oregano salt and pepper high simmer forty-five
minutes serve over cheese ravioli just-picked greens
for salad the blonde weekend anchorwoman who
took a leave of absence to have a baby is back still
no word on the trapped miners and a story that is
sure to warm your heart Frankie writes he's at a
national flute convention in Albuquerque wishing

he was dead he's no longer mad at me for the things I said about his wife Latinos grill meat burning fat sizzles smoke into the air smell seasoned flesh on fire Spanish music on the radio ninety degrees humid mushrooms need good soaking rains followed by clear cool temperatures soon chanterelles followed by boletes and oyster then the divine hen-of-the-woods Amanda writes Herb Pomeroy dead Herb who blew "Making Whoopie" as she and James walked down the aisle sweet Herb of blowing brass love hard to get up groggy little bits of love find their way in the man you fear is across the street waves and you wave back breakfast with old high school girlfriend Ann who lives in Vermont on an old farm sewing king size bed sheet American flags lettered with hand-sewn writing her husband a potter makes pots that look like limbs that grow grass they see deer bear and long winters Healey School meet new secretary Mary same woman who books substitute teachers the voice I have known for many years talk with Mrs. Harris about PTA will you sub this fall dishwasher still broke wash by hand Julia dries puts them away trying to finish last collage of summer mushroom teepee spoon moon bird clown pond can't get enough space into it put aside sort through piles of handouts find student poem printed on purple paper titled "Forgotten" the sun warms my shoulders as I zigzag through the sea of humans down the street it is the thought of a girl I had seen on the Orange Line that floats in my mind there's forty to fifty of them at a time why do I always find my eyes falling on the breasts of naked manikins Celeste's head bobs on waves in the pool wide smile goggled and buoyant she and Julia swim across the pool and back I sit pool's edge legs in water self-conscious my sagging flesh and bad gums Max Roach dead finally reunited with Clifford Brown not so new family living in the house behind us has new dog barking in the yard since five this morning Molly and I walk the bike path behind Julia and Celeste on their bikes J.P. Licks for an ice cream sit on bench next to Molly the girls play out among the statues in Davis Square Julia remembers the time in winter she threw a snowball landed right on a male statue's garbanzos standing alone for the moment on my own concrete island the location of the Boston Massacre long before Interstate 93 or Milk Row for that matter this is known as always massacres downtown the windows at Filene's smell perfume walk through the door nearly fifty years ago Christmas my mother my older sister and my younger sister Santa Ed is right about Kevin White Whitey Fanny Howe and the Virgin Mary but he's twisting things around with regards to Bill I'm just happy to get my name in the book any book even one not as great as Ed's can use my name *To the*

Lighthouse Halibut Point look north to Plum Island
and Maine kids hold a long boa albino corn snakes
timber rattler copperhead no I wouldn't like to touch
it then the ascent down to the sea along the impos-
ing quarry high jagged granite walls fifty foot drop
to jade blue water wind fierce off ocean walk down
through stunted woods and brush smash of waves
on rock Avery Julia Gavin Seamus Celeste Veronica
Abigail Sam Charlie explore ancient crevices climb
boulder formations get too close to the water hey
get down from there hey don't get so close to the
water put your sneakers back on you can't climb
rocks barefoot barely enough time to talk past chat
what with kid interruptions Amanda James Jim Arian
Gerrit Patrick all the time an eye on the kids the
other on the choppy sea brave sailboat way out dis-
tances I can't reconcile the sailboat is out too far
good to see you it's been too long and Patrick lived
one summer in a tent not far from here Amanda
went to see Willie Alexander and shook it up like
getting change out of a parking meter kissed Willie
made him blush Gerrit and several others once
skinny dipped in the quarry and fried clams at clam
shack anyone ever seen a heart-shaped rock it's
empty inside like tokens on a coffin or make-up on
a corpse the soul of a Boston poet language and
Dorchester Bay what is buried under UMass Boston
maybe there's another reason the underground

parking garages closed permanently they say the buildings are caving in on them perhaps something else slinks towards Beantown to be killed and disposed of in an not-so-efficient manner they admitted a crazy old man who's just been thrown off another unit for being too violent even though her unit is already full this guy needs one on one so that puts them down one from the start for the past three weeks Sunday morning seven o'clock they're doing masonry work on the three-family owned by the old lady who's been dying bedridden now haven't seen her in weeks this man and woman at times like they're brother and sister other times like they're married she's butch maybe fifty short hair wears shorts tank top and work boots he's a stocky man bald and indifferent to her constant barking Joey are you sure that's going to fit Joey you're going to need a bigger blade Joey where did you put the hammer Joey you're going to need more cement Joey I'd put more than that on Joey why don't you start on the other side Joey works his way around the house with his ancient artistry stone work cement work brick work Joey make it nice and the Indian family big brown house three doors down grandparents in traditional attire their children their children's children carrying Trader Joe's bags from the car to the back stairs I think the new owners of the house behind us rent rooms and do laundry for money there's always guys coming and going not always the same faces sometimes with bags of laundry leaving them and picking them up the woman who seems to be the matron is a middle-aged Latino woman a few younger men I recognize who live there maybe her sons the important things I learn in the head I forget in the heart in rainy Somerville private morning writing time closes with a letter I'll be seeing you before we know it as time passes like water got to go now the girls are stirring and I've got to get them breakfast leftover pasta with sauce for Julia taquitos for Celeste love Joe the man the mountain the reptile the new mouse in house soon as the weather turns cool early nester it's not wrong to be numb to the war they have been at war since I was born and thousands years ago and two hundred years they were at war they won the war of 1612 lost in 1727 fifteen hundred years ago they tied and split it down the middle they started the war then ended the war they lost one war because they were late you can't run a war on Shadow Time that transcends past present and future they need standard time one o'clock on the dot shoot the missile you want war the Chinese poets knew war don't tell Li Po shit about war sometimes I don't know who my friends are it's not that I don't trust my friends I don't trust myself no you won't find much sex in my new book pick up cut brush sweep patio clean the front porch store kids summer stuff in the basement except for the bikes yes except for the bikes still to be done before end of summer paint railing and new front steps forms to fill out for the department handouts to print syllabus to revise nephew's wedding and niece's birthday party tomatoes everywhere basil too sliced tomatoes with sardines tomato pepper and cucumber salad marinara sauce tomato with fresh mozzarella and basil salad eat one like an apple put in cheese sandwich slice in spinach salad baked stuffed or fried gazpacho cold pasta and tomato salad he gives me a jar of what looks like pee it's some brew he ferments from yeast they drink in parts of Russia where they consume daily doses of vodka smoke cigarettes live to be a hundred and twenty take a few ounces in the morning it's a digestive of sorts tastes like mild vinegar in the middle of yoga positions I am forced to the bathroom I try to convince myself that it's okay if I don't paint the new front stairs and railings maybe I'm fooling myself living in the city why not a move away with a little land a garden and slow my life down o Ed tell me an interminable story like the one about the older man who leaves his wife to follow Joe College's slender form or the boxer who fought under his mother's maiden name I've got a pair of scissors and a jar of glue that's what I do when I sit here feeling that I fail my family cut and paste it's hardly rocket science a child can do it how to justify stealing time away for child's play this is known as guilt when you can't find words you stutter this is how our hearts break watching people we love hurting and nobody can say a thing she forgets how many days she was away to visit my sister thinks we just got back from our vacation no Ma we got back weeks ago where was it you went oh New York that's where Dad and I went on our honeymoon did the kids have a good time when did you get back she believes she goes to day care to volunteer I help the old people there's a lot of them with canes or wheelchairs one of the ladies she always says to me thank you for all your help and we exercise and they have stories and yesterday or one day I can't remember if it was Monday or anyway this man came and he played what do you call an instrument the guitar it wasn't the guitar but it was I can't remember and I asked one of the ladies what is that he's playing and I went to visit your sister was busy when I went there and I didn't like the food I was hungry but I didn't like the food kids straighten their room I catch up on laundry school begins next week make sure all their clothes and supplies in order dry and fold vacuum still no dishwasher constant flow of dishes silverware and glasses coffee mugs pans call repair man tomorrow read with Celeste chess with Julia Celeste takes on the winner the unity of body and mind is an industry look at poor Greece it's like *The Inferno* I can't find my way out of a train station up stairs down elevators onto platforms miss trains as I open a stairway door out walks the Latino woman who lives behind me she sees me I see her we both look the other way like we don't know we're neighbors we're in the country steep hills rise around us the house is not what Molly wants walk half a day down mountain road until a bus drives us to a little town divided by a paved road and a stream meanders its way under occasional bridges when we get to the car someone stole my acoustic guitar smashed the window last of the raspberries hard and tart broccoli turning out slower and smaller lettuce small but tasty peppers with little flavor chard and kale producing sauté with garlic and olive oil serve with pasta butter and cheese eat last of my birthday cake carrot wash kitchen blinds with cleaner years grease covered by layers of dust mop kitchen floor home then is one place where humans can realize a part or their dignity the daily jottings I write orphans and heard and tread creatures be kind to men brotherly children insects rejoice at life then herbs men merits and trees with compassionate goodness display humiliation bear no grudge thousands aspire higher delight the ones the ones the ones they rebel against should reason they injure no concur no injure they attack and punish those less superior they curry heaven's information slanderous and stubborn agitate vowels they lie seize they wrong divination chase positions they correct craft slay disregard wholly submissive they bribes heavy deride close up they straight reason obstruct they save eggs and fresh power waste destroy goods valuables good property with unbridled private desire marriage grow rich they in others vulgar no shame no glory they short maybe five-two recognize favors ceremony they disturb thereby demand property spoil seeing they resist make raids find fault instruct tricks rail at borrow with hearts cast aside vindicate gently brag jump over children husbands wives sing on the correct days they face north naked point at crimes heinous controllers spit fire at seasonal festivals burn execute according to cause filthy calling faggots and failing moon and gravity my heart awakens the appliance repair man calls he's running behind be later than he thinks what's wrong with the dishwasher it won't work Sunday gravy with meatballs this is the recipe I got from you she says oh you wrote it down no Ma from sitting in the kitchen with all those Sunday mornings and you'd have me strain the tomatoes and go out to the garden and pick basil and let me have a meatball out of the frying pan even though I just had breakfast most of what I cook is the same food you cooked oh well at least I was good for something macaroni followed by meat and salad orange sorbet quiet walk down the street the girls ahead of us they're so beautiful Joe and did I tell you my friend Mary said once she said what did they go and bring those kids from another country for well there's a lot of ignorance and hate in the world well she doesn't like anyone anyway Jews or colored people smell decomposing leaves look to the ground dead leaves it's only the first of September we stand at the end of the driveway wave goodbye as the senior citizens van pulls away Julia Celeste and Abigail drink grape soda out of old-fashioned bottles James plays with Sam Amanda and I sit on the bench Gloucester gossip and the different ways of looking at our mothers slip away the neighbors behind us put a brick and stone patio over the space the old owner used as a garden a wheelbarrow stands on the spot where they filled in the fish pond the wheelbarrow is filled with fine sand morning glories wind around the patio up over the rose bush twist around the wrought iron porch railings spread up cling to climbing ivy on the side of the house sweet grape taste in the air neighbor's vines laden with plump purple-blue clusters last of the tomatoes slice big one top with sardines oregano salt and pepper eat with good bread first week of classes this is what the course is this is what we'll do this is how we'll do it this is what is expected of you nephew's wedding the band is two lesbians one on acoustic and vocals the other on tenor sax playing '70s soft rock isn't the view nice how's the lobster nice doesn't the bride look nice her daughter is very nice personally I think her mom is nice sun and moon in sky Julia and I clean out my studio and the little room behind water's been getting in moldy sponge cakes sprout from linoleum throw out two boxes of trash organize paintings and painting desk paints brushes boxes of little cut out pieces unfinished collage sits on the desk last pieces waiting for me to paste in place clear writing desk shelve dozens of books sweep and vacuum floor walk down the trail parts snowed in other parts wind-blown down rocks descend from the high country wander into the back of someone's yard they're fishing where the water rushes fast and violent from under a dam he pulls out a fish that has an amphibious head then wide awake worry about the girls worry about my mother waving goodbye driving off in the van alone some desire a bigger house years ago at parties I was first to be unsteady on my feet and what have I learned all these years trying to be a man who could sit in one moment and say that heaven's music is poetry and chant under a street lamp Julia cuts paper in the little room snorting and sniffing home from school this be my material today September 12 2007 first mushroom walk of the season still holding to summer green the trees throw long shadows tips of leaves brushed rust-pink Sparky bounds ahead circles behind woods dry not enough rain July and August mushrooms will be hard to come by down to the edge of the reservoir past the Keep Out and threat of prosecution sign walk around out of the way inlet under white pines climb the Reservoir Trail up over knoll down into granite cut over wooden footbridge bushwhack back down check out the edge of the swampy stuff not a fungus to be found turn up Skyline Trail slow uphill big hawk swoops over from behind startles us settles high on the branch of an old oak tree Sparky rears barks the bird remains statue still for a moment then gracefully departs over the forest I don't know my hawks Dan Bouchard could identify that bird here the dying old lady in the three-decker next door is being cared for by hospice people they come and go change of shift for the first time in weeks she's in the wheelchair on the front porch with a young hospice worker who yells everything she says because the lady has lost her hearing o hawk in the big oak tree Amanda writes that she cried driving through the tunnel red jello spilled into the sky and splattered the back seat risotto with mushrooms caramelized onions and spinach people come and go in uniforms on hospital beds in cars and trucks that cut you off how by some different fate they could be people that you love like the old woman who talks to you in the supermarket line she drank her sorrows away felt shitty the next day driving around in a '67 Dodge Dart listening to Iggy and the Stooges who wouldn't fall in love with her piles of scraps littering the kitchen floor or how the breezes blow uncertain as the day wavers yesterday's unopened mail will she or won't she open windows to the morning air how's your mother is she any better no she isn't she's not going to get any better either in some areas the first frost can be expected the girls do homework Sparky asleep on his bed Molly working at the hospital load of laundry in the dryer another in the washer several loads on deck chicken soup this afternoon Julia says make a big batch Dad will you be available to substitute this year no I won't be available to substitute this year yes I will continue on as corresponding secretary of the PTA yes I will come in and do poetry yes I can come and be a guest speaker for the poetry and performance club he wandered extensively in his home at times the distance between himself and the center was overwhelming Julia explains how leaves of the tomato plants are poisonous Celeste names the planets in the solar system is Jupiter still considered a planet I thought by now it had become a Catholic Cardinal she needs to have a drink and loosen up if Niedecker doesn't like being a house cleaner why doesn't she do something else from the student who in every poem alludes to men calling her beautiful first day of fall temperatures in the 80s still no rain the woods dry mushrooms non-existent carcass of a fly-infested possum she caught a seven-legged spider in a cup and left him outside some days I actually think I am good but my horoscope warns against getting comfortable what else am I doing wrong I ask myself the love we put into things we can never get it back I seek to add to the History of the Parting of the Way in ancient times this was known as adding to the History of the Parting of the Way she is a strange misty form like vapor passing into the being of others while they pass within her and become her guests our shapes and limbs our words and thoughts jostle and run into each other a stranger shifts tongues without leaving your home she knows everything under the sky without look-ing out her window she knows that the farther one travels the less one knows she arrives without going sees without looking in doing nothing achieves everything in watching her die she knows all there is to know about life under harvest moon warm humid temperatures possible record high she was attacked by an escaping guerilla now her parents are suing I keep forgetting dreams that I tell myself I will remember I am in a speed boat I can be sure there's the city of Boston always the same city of Boston in my dreams or do I think that while dreaming you think you're so cool and I've seen that high school couple every day now for weeks he carries her on his back I've tried to keep sex out of this but one of my students wrote a poem in the manner of Williams so much depends upon the red dildo glazed with lube beside the nice pussy I didn't write it she did so go yell at her standing at the gate of the Temple of the Holier Than Thou await the ringing bell where I will eat white rice and steamed vegetables I would love to cook a meal for you a good autumn feast roast rabbit with wild mushrooms braised shanks of beef lots of good wine I can't remember half what I've read in books but I remember television shows from the sixties every episode every series the one where Beaver befriends the hobo what if I'd been chanting all those years instead of absorbing Andy of Mayberry and *Bewitched* chanting an eternal mantra of all mantra in the name of mantras in ancient times they were known as mantra and handed down to the special ones I have one to this day but I can't tell you because it's a personal thing okay I'll tell you it's Om Oxt Asanataia in the state retirement plan I have to put in twenty years as half-time teacher to get retirement benefits so if I continue to teach I'll be seventy-two when I can earn minimum benefits and if you're wife dies before you or if you die before your wife and the life policy comes automatic if you go this way you get the four point three percent there that one all depends on the market if you work full time or three-quarter time even some of the time you can buy more time you get the dental automatic even if you are on your wife's use it first and then you're wife's second is all this making any sense the main thing you need to think about now is which retirement plan is best for you so I work twenty more years to make a couple of hundred bucks a month and with social security I can drool into my shirt and eat canned food products I have no vision of a condo in Florida golf and gulf shrimp stories of partying in cars and love gone sour and one night stands and watching friends die and two people walking down a windy pavilion as the trees sway side to side with leaves falling in a hypnotizing matter from left to right and Mary and Jack drink lemonade on the beach what's wrong Jack nothing Mary the stench of cigarette smoke hangs in the tiny car I don't want to lose you yeah let's go I feel a sense of indescribable positivity but I feel uncomfortable around you me I'm cool you sure why wouldn't I be it's just that I never met anybody like you before the car goes silent not another word is said just leave me alone Meg please aren't you going to stop the blood hell of an ice breaker you're too nice Tarzan hit me with a beer brah don't you know the way of course baby there is so much that I want to say that I need to say can she even hear me this is it if you want to say goodbye you'd better come in now o life and death in letters never trust a poet who uses o in a poem like o life o death or o whatever fill it in yourself which I learned about from reading the ancient text The Book of Misery O Whatever Fill It In Yourself clouds throw shadows across the laptop strong eastern wind cool it down bring wet ground three of them struggle to get her down the stairs in the wheelchair lift her skeleton into the car only a dilapidated head left and the face of death they watch her die I watch her die and I watch her watch her mother die I watch my mother die though my mother's not dying in a physical sense when their mother dies they get the house right now the market's not good there's houses for sale all over Somerville not selling maybe now they want to keep her alive until the market gets better today she tries not to think of her mother dying Amanda writes she reads translations in the tub while everyone is asleep where does she fit into the elbows and wool enough to simply let things go to seed birds love it the mustard and thistle Julia says Buddha rides a manta ray and loves it you don't have to try and make rhyme and meter well I went to a Catholic high school the birds get lots of mileage out of this warm weather really no way to describe a bird's call whistle tweak chirp they don't sound like the sounds the birds actually make right now out the window one in particular chirp every two and a half seconds and lots of other higher and lower pitched and timing and delivery who knows what the birds know this is known as knowing you never know what the birds know so I go she says I don't know how many maybe it's I'm not sure Tuesdays I think it's once a week I go there when did I go there Betty drops me and they take the van they drop them off I can walk it's right down the street but oh no you come in the van he's a nice man the man who drives the van they're all old people I help them where I can in their wheelchairs who has a cane I was there yesterday was it yesterday I don't know and then I have my friend Mary she comes we go out to lunch but she'll call me when she's going to come it might be today is today Friday what are you doing in opposition to the war I'm writing a book about freedom the brick patio half finished in the yard behind us already the bricks are off level and it's sinking in the center someone's out there with a leaf blower blowing the leaves around I'm sorry I've been late for class but I'm a manic depressive and my medication makes me sleep late three in the morning unable to sleep woken by animals screeching outside raccoon and possum perhaps Sparky wakes the house running around downstairs barking the animals apparently fighting now it stops my mind won't so what pension plan is the best and where did the check for the kids' science camp go put a stop payment write a new one finish one pile of student papers begin another stack twenty years thousands poems thousands short stories thousands insightful responses then you get this pension but it won't be much so maybe you should go with the 401B the advantage being it's portable that leaf blower's louder than a chainsaw drowning everything but a boy's shout on his way home from school too cool for this world this boy the key for me is not to look at the clock if I look at the clock and know the time it'll be two hours at least until I'm back asleep if it's four and I look I'm basically up for the day since I rise at six so I chant trying to put the breaks on the electricity slow my mind down this is where you live is a great last line for a poem I heard Ed read from *Kevin White* at PA's Lounge I fully understood the implications of body dumpster and Holy Trinity Bill Corbett would hate Bill Lee because Bill Lee boasted of eating pot pancakes and nearly smuggled a batch into Charlie's Kitchen where he planned to get Bill Corbett stoned there's a body there's a body everywhere's a body they found human bones for sale at a flea market road work's got traffic locked Union Square Somerville Ave. spills over into Cambridge bulldozers dump trucks backhoes steam rollers cops stand and chat with construction workers pay no mind to the five- and ten-minute stops half hour to drive the mile home from Harvard Square Ange writes that she's tired of poets who write about their lives and things like motherhood dying grandparents and memorable sunsets is that all there is she wants to know but that's not all there is friends can die mothers can die or you can have a cloudy day and can't see the sun setting maybe you're a father forced to write about fatherhood I wash and fold two loads girls' clothes there's two more loads I shout you're killing me with the laundry and go on a five-minute tirade about how long it takes to wash and fold four loads and how much water it takes and electricity half the stuff they throw in isn't even dirty then I apologize for yelling sun isn't setting it's shooting across this screen and I can't see these words I write last evening when the sun set Davis Square golden orange painted the basketball court and the six guys playing pickup lit up why quote other writers artists theorists philosophers instead of saying it yourself is that all there is is one of those songs that you make fun of and it's been ruined and overused like Beatles songs but it's actually a dark song hello this is John Ashbery have you driven a Lincoln lately and now it comes as I wonder will the old lady next door die before the book ends Kevin dies before the book ends Kevin sixteen in '79 rockabilly haircut dirty jeans engineer boots Kevin we sneak you into the Cantab to see Mission of Burma Kevin of late night

jams every Velvet's song ever written I guess just
don't know Kevin of punk bands I'll be okay don't
worry it won't be that hard of sweat lodge and sky
high hawk vision of poison snake ring bells and
chant how long hold her hand play a song Kevin
ring a bell for Mary old temple Great Wall how long
now that's great can you be not here first fuck on
back stairs in Billerica seasick on charter boat you
going to eat your lunch back streets of Wuhan you
can't stay at the monastery what would I tell your
mother that's a great shirt you me and Jay naked in
one bed only fan in the house blows on us three pigs
in a blanket are you really not here is it that bad you
can't do that this God how God where God when did
you and how at my wedding you looked so fucking
cool my dumb-fuck father thought you were
retarded Celeste says she feels bad you look so
handsome in that tuxedo Rocket Rocket record
photo you in '50s convertible top down James Dean
indeed light candles meditate The Ramones didn't
change the world but believing is everything the Vir-
gin Mary is with John Wieners if you find anyone
answering their description please let me know what
lives on in my heart is you wounds tombs and
bombs Kevin in a Stupa garden Mr. Jin is the confi-
dence man I read about him in Melville asleep on
the hardwood floor why you do it why you do it
remember the Regal Beagle and body surfing at Sal-

isbury Beach this is where you live this is where you live in the woods in the foothills in the Adirondacks make music chant sit in your sweat lodge let visions come your life a short walk to the pond cook a good meal sit down and eat come visit us for the weekend it's been too long she's still alive they've got her out on the front porch Celeste Julia and I walk the stream's edge step into the water chase trout upstream into a shallow pool the way the Indians catch them with our hand Dad these are mammals trouble brewing over a mock witch hanging where to buy your pumpkins Kevin's father's brother dies so Kevin's father loses a son and brother in less than a week my neighbor Elizabeth isn't answering her door so her landlord my neighbor Lucy walks upstairs and finds her dead Dear Amanda melted butter coats the yeasty dough balls a red-headed woodpecker in front of me flying from tree to tree Sparky make good company through the swamp and thick tangles Sparky struggles to make in and around briars tear at my jeans feet ankle deep into muck no mushrooms in here this year no mush-rooms anywhere except the farmer who sells hen-of-the-woods and chicken mushrooms at the farmer's market I'm forced to buy this year sauté in butter pound and a half cleaned cut hen-of-the-woods pinch of salt freezer pack separate containers for winter risottos stews sauces gravies or omelets

Dear Amanda I get the feeling your book may never end in the old days this was known as cutting weeds planting trees Dear Tao even you are a liar and I spit in your face twice it was October a bright wispy day as I walked slowly up the stairs to think about dinner would I could I should I be a gentleman skilled in the business of life the bird outside my window mocks me do you think there's anything to the dreaming of the sleeper tale on sale Neil says children suck how can you hate children but Neil does he hates everything and moving away to live on an island there'll be less to hate Dear Frank every time I try to leave a message your voice box is full you spend your weeks at flute conventions in Kansas you eat fatty foods and drink too much you stroke it like seventeen you take painful shits your hemorrhoids swell and burn you bleed you cry you son of Megara you can suddenly learn to knit birds make the most of browned sunflowers sliver and gold slivers and antique buttons I love you mother crying trying to keep up too many things to do I can't remember the last time I washed the bed sheets the house is cold wear layers leek and potato soup hey little girl you don't have to hide nothing no more I can't even mop the kitchen floor layers of dirt dust spilled food and drink walked over stepped on an abstract charcoal on wood-grain canvas time to have my blood checked fast from midnight next morning Broadway Health Clinic friendly woman I make note of her being friendly because the previous couple of years the woman drawing blood was a cold hostile nosey woman would start scolding me soon as I walked though the door who told you to come here let me see your forms why are you having blood drawn sit down there intimidating bursts never allowing me to compose myself then bang she took pleasure in the big jab the older kid hands the pistol off to the younger kid can't be more than eight and he places the gun inside the waist of his pants and covers it with his shirt he can't be more than eight they start even younger than that what are sniper's numbers what does sniper mean what do Marines mean peace means numbers and snipers babies and children parents and dead children numbers dead children and love and dead children and numbers peace and love I don't give a shit about baseball or the World Series is there really a new crop of peas temperatures in the 70s and 80s whole chicken in fresh herbs garlic and lemon roast serve with spinach and brown rice they're boyfriends and girlfriends suicide tragic car accidents smoking dope and moving away from some shit hole they were born in and men beating women girls being girls boys being boys boys beating boys hospitals and bloodied doctors bearing bad news addiction the miracle of living innocence and innocence lost dying in dreams she asks should I like make my characters into like werewolves or like vampires why would you want to do that because like it would be like fun mop the kitchen floor do dishes three loads of laundry she wants to be a writer and teach creative writing I'm going to read political poems he says looking to the audience for approval which they readily offer she reads from her prize-winning novel about sex and electricity so fucking bored I think what can I eat later Dear Everybody after New Year's I will not attend readings until further notice please don't take it personally I have nothing left to give Dear Jim Behrle kill kill kill those who advertise the poem out may they be forced to work the fields for a piece of bread a day the Siamese amphibious creature tears at its heads with long sharp teeth until one head finally falls off he throws it in the water the human body is the image of the conflict between two states the entire natural world consists of a network of secret correspondences Celeste tries to teach her how to play Sorry Nanna you're doing it wrong Dear Novel you cannot contain me go fuck yourself my mother phones did Molly get the check I sent for her birthday no well I sent it a week ago maybe you put the wrong address no I didn't I have your address why would I put the wrong address chocolate mocha cake for Molly's birthday bottle of white French Burgundy Molly makes a crown for Celeste's

queen costume Julia models her Black Death cos-
tume two pumpkins to carve then trick or treat
down the street en route home from playing music
in Groton cheesy-yellow moon plays peek-a-boo
with clouds against black and blue night sky above
Acton and Concord along Route 2 big deer bright
eyes by the side of the road and two big bucks my
neighbor slays with his bow each with bloody holes
where the arrow pierced flesh you can survey your
entire life looking into such holes the alphabets of
all languages reveal traces of ancient characters they
beat the boy senseless over neighborhood turf but
one of the beaters has a conscience and a sense of
moral responsibility aware that there is a world
beyond neighborhood and words in which the dead
appear in the form of animals if you could swallow
your tail you could pass the time rather than waste
it o earthly figures clouds and musical notes the PTA
does not have enough money for all the field trips
parents are urged to donate what they can if you
cannot donate money please donate your time it's
not that I'm elitist she says I just want my kid to have
every advantage possible this must be a dream I tell
myself wake up but my mother and I stranded on
high rugged terrain try to find safe way down all
avenues of descent too steep for her you go Joe I'll
stay here finally wake body shakes unable to fall
back to sleep five-thirty rise make coffee and Molly's

lunch get breakfast ready for the girls Julia scrapes
season's first frost off windshield Central Street traf-
fic backed up from Highland to Broadway drop girls
off at school order Thanksgiving turkey Amanda
writes broken water main no dishes no baths brown
water leaves ring in sink bodies and trinkets faces
that look the same delirious after hours in one room
say you are sorry hearing I am sorry and being sorry
the way make-up cakes at the edge of a bullet hole
tonight the moon is a yellow shock above the Brazil-
ian church on School Street Dear Cousin Joe
attached a photo of the elk I killed in New Mexico
eight hundred pound creature long broad antlers
three bullet holes closely grouped above its shoulder
dead beast against vast hilly land Biblical rains cut
gullies in the driveway vacuum Sparky's white hair
caked into the blue living room carpet who of us
exemplifies a devotion to Nature and spontaneity at
all costs comes out formlessly fashioned by electrical
currents and words whose kingdom's weedy
meadow far-star plant life I can't stop needing
anchorwoman blue-eyed BC graduate you cheer
you cheer for your team teary-eyed blond say good-
bye to your wholesome boy-man anchorman Notre
Dame graduate you cheer you cheer for your team
ten years six o'clock in the morning Paula Ebben and
Chris Wahle two of you and an escaped gorilla from
Franklin Park Zoo who will take your place Chris

find out after the break not yet mid-November already the Christmas music decorations everywhere I wonder what would happen if the Atheists had a yearly holiday with Atheistmas decorations and Atheistmas Carols and Merry Atheistmas and Happy New Year oh dear you'd fear Dear Joe wisdom says that when one needs nurturing one can find nurturing in nurturing Dear Wisdom-Fart the Wisdom that can be named is not the true Wisdom one day I climbed a tall hill overlooking Interstate 93 drank wine played music until some young thugs appeared sizing me up one of them asked did I have any money before I could answer a stray kite flew above us and dropped a mouldy rat which hit that boy in the head suddenly they reeled and scattered Julia eats clam chowder for breakfast Celeste cereal six whole wheat Fig Newtons for me cup of strong coffee he told me to use the things of the world to cultivate Tao I walk being careful of the cobblestones beneath my noticeably artificial feet me with unspeakable fashion faux pas I totally heard you you don't like me there's nothing I can do about it I am not such a caricature pussyfooting along wearing sunglasses heck of a tale anyways I called him he never called back Jack be oldie Jack be goldie Jack come round on the merry go-hold-me we'll pause in front of bookstores invite the shop keepers out to lunch sleazy as our stature will allow we'll look through stacks of old volumes mindful not to breathe too heavily oh don't bring an axe murderer into the story have you listened to a fucking thing I've said this semester I have had no contact for days now I fit into my old jeans I had been called a sexy conservative more than twice did they expect I would go running back these are the bits and pieces of information they have been handing me for the past three days she let the pedophile go after one of the girls ran but it's a true story morning showers give way to bright sun here after class down muddy hill to the parking lot jets roar in and out of Logan white caps on the bay quick run down 93 to Rt. 28 exit down under the highway snake up McGrath and O'Brien right onto Medford Street make the light and Alpine and the one at School left down School first right on Oxford first driveway on the left little brown and beige house in the back you walk right past and won't notice Dear Professor I broke up with my girlfriend today and I think I broke my hand so I won't make it to class dishwater not working again I could have replaced it by now poverty sneaks up behind you in the form of green liquid brewed by swamp moms the funeral procession moves so slowly as if to stop time never does go as it might in a white-washed room where you wander and reflect upon strained dreams and floppy ears here's where steers move around no more rough and tough stuff

Spam on white not even mustard art's overrated says the guy in the café it's got nothing to do with the poor those museums full of Campbell soup cans stones and other ugly things I love the smell of skin right after a shower sirens outside the house between breath and no breath work until eight at night everyone speaks in smoke mothers walk by smile nod make certain their hair is straight these parents younger by decades and the bell and the kids burst through the door the pavement shines inscription reads benevolent smile upon the sidewalk your blue clarity speaks warm browns reply they hold their signs with determination Julia kicks the ball to me I kick it to Celeste she kicks it to Julia and so it goes I play goalie and Julia and Celeste try to score on me Julia says she has superiority over us because soccer is a matter of mathematic propositions since she's better at math she has the upper hand I run and kick out of breath play announcer Dad are you going to play goal or announce the game but here comes Celeste last chance of the game she's got the breakaway will Pop be able to stop her no she scores Celeste scores the winning goal and the crowd is going wild and make a noise through my cupped hands to sound like a crowd sometimes I don't feel like seeing anyone not friends not acquaintances better the brood who played lute well who ran out of provisions while traveling east

the two brothers one valued life the other didn't
man who swam six directions in four seas his body
became accord with his mind the clever little child
later suffered from abnormality when he grew up
the young woman who lived in a remote hut tried
to find the Way but died of a broken heart sweep
leaves clear brush clean the front porch get rid of
the tire that's been sitting there for six months today
fifty poems to read then end of the semester portfo-
lios post grades Sun Salutations at sunrise keep my
body stretched and limber birds pick over last of the
grapes quarter moon between the two big pines sun
and moon Julia says sun brushes gold pine boughs
sharp moon sliver cuts bluing sky so hand me that
drug of Roman origin and say the Drug of Roman
Origin is not the real Drug we drank mint juleps but
lost our connection men with pipes trying to write
fugues who said they wouldn't fondle a saint the
turkey is dead sitting in the refrigerator turkey sour-
dough bread sausage and cranberry stuffing gravy
mashed potatoes roasted sweet potatoes good bread
cranberry sauce mixed green salad glazed carrots
Molly's apple pie and cookies for dessert who do we
thank and why do we thank and who would have
thought guy who moved in the second floor of the
three-decker long gray hair and beard huge belly
sips beer from cans with a straw wears a jacket with
a large Marines patch on the back drives a jeep with

zebra seat covers Gus and Maria new roof and gutters men climb ladders walk so surely on dangerous roof pitch three horror novels Julia three science books Celeste and on walk home from library full moon rise while opposite sky cinnamon sun one in the morning rise for piss room cold vent blowing chilly air downstairs basement to furnace try to light the pilot but no-go call someone in the morning but it's Sunday morning who will come wrapped in blankets wide awake read Bill's "Whalen Poems" Snowball escapes from the cage Snowball the white hamster we're babysitting Celeste Julia and Molly all awake put on gloves wrap my hands gently around Snowball place him back in cage hello my name is Joe Torra and my phone number and our furnace died could someone come out on Sunday and yes for a hundred-fifty emergency fee Mike shows up mid-morning gets the heater going bypasses something says he'll come back tomorrow with the part he bypassed and fix it permanently which he does Mike just left with a four hundred dollar check and Molly's computer's crashed we're sharing this one three loads of the girls' laundry load of sheets load of my stuff the old house in Medford and we walk down Park Street to Hickey Park go into Ma's store she buys me an ice cream cone but Ma's doesn't sell ice cream cones she sells slush we walk to the park sit on a bench eat our ice cream Dad will be here soon she says I say Dad is dead what are you talking about he's not dead why would you say that I say because Dad is dead we sit there way past dark all the kids go home a few teenagers I recognize huddle in the surrounding blackness he chases me into a supermarket I keep him away knocking over displays cans and boxes hit his face and draw blood the market is crowded people back away hold their breath I trip up against the canned fish shelf and fall he wields his gun has a henchmen tie my hands while another goes for plastic bags then he covers my head with a plastic bag I'm trying to get enough plastic between my teeth so that I can bite a hole to breathe Dear Mr. Torra I'd like to talk with you about my short story I'm stuck it's the one about the girl's life from childbirth through college Dear Herman Melville why did you wave your hand at me three times in that funny way even the Music Master follows behind you who told me that the guy he worked for tried to hit on him and what to cook for Christmas dinner in olden times there was fish to fry on Christmas Eve salt cod calamari eels spaghetti with anchovy and garlic shrimp vinegar peppers stuffed with bread pinch of anchovy and now she only makes tea for herself last week left the water running again it flooded the downstairs who ever gets to sing their lover to sleep should keep a close watch on this heart of mine November temperature mid-thirties saw a kid run out into the traffic and nearly get run over the new pot-bellied neighbor with the long gray hair and beard who sips beer through a straw works for the T I see him at the Davis Square Station the smell of burning plastic brought him out of his gloomy nostalgia and after swimming out in the wild river he entered the vortex of the inflow and left with the outflow o heavenly wings of the cicada restore my own state to look with your ears listen with your eyes breakfast Celeste scrambled eggs Julia leftover baked ziti drop them off at school coffee with Neil at the café Neil three times married not counting ex-girlfriends crazy client that owes him money for a case now she's in a state hospital where they put you if you let on to what you are really thinking two inches snow followed by sleet then rain six in the morning shovel heavy slush clean Molly's car off to work Julia down with the cold that Molly and Celeste had keep her home call the absent line drive Celeste to school kids in snow boots winter jackets snowballs forever cars spin on slick road-tops I started reading the novel about the three hundred masters who found transcendence and became legends but too many months passed then winter and those novels long-winded by the time Wang Ch'ung-yang tested Ch'ang-ch'un I put the book down and never picked it up again I know there was a fire and they all ended

up living in the Greatest House still to this day con-
sidered one of the top fifty great houses o Master I
cried and you have not answered from this time on
the immigrants came in throngs long lines and they
want to put up walls what if we can't get out I'm
growing tired of discussing God and affairs of the
world I didn't notice that Amanda cut her hair until
the poetry reading in Lowell because of an over-
abundance of females it says that the primary focus
of the story is to regard female children more highly
and to this end the model of the family is presented
but this is not to suggest that girls should be valued
as highly or treated the same as boys in this life or
after their death or in the world of the spirits in the
first two months of the lunar year the silkworms are
about to emerges do short stories really have Dear
Professor Torra could you write me a letter of rec-
ommendation Hey Joe do you want to come up and
play music this week Dear Valued Customer your
order has been shipped no need to leave the house
to holiday shop what pigs we have made of our-
selves in ancient times this was known as people
making pigs of themselves the new morning anchor-
man is more of a wimp than the old pan sear short
ribs sauté garlic and ground turkey add tomatoes
ribs parsley oregano salt and pepper slowly simmer
until the meat shreds from the bone Molly's new job
after all these years out of patient care to the desk

side of healthcare no more shitty assholes bring down Christmas decorations presents coming in the mail big and little boxes on the front porch no Santa here just men in uniforms cold brown boxes don't open anything that's for Molly those for me First Alert Doppler says it'll stay on the cold side late breaker tanker overturns at the Route 16 Route 99 rotary cars and houses on fire we called it Condelli Curve because it's the spot where Danny Condelli ran the rotary a bit too fast and flipped his old Triumph Danny Condelli who picked on me eighth grade scared shit I called him out one day having had enough beat him bloody until his sidekick Fran D'Amico begged me to let him go he's my friend he said then it hit me what I'd done blood all over right hand enough abdominal breathing every inhale every exhale every claim that the whales had nothing to do with Melville's march to the river and possibilities of selves and selves of others curses the soul of a riverboat queen go become pious and obedient my bad traits multiply by nines to protective talismans black ink on rice paper don't kill don't steal don't don't don't don't roar large jet en route to Logan ooh that sounds like a big one Daddy Tornado the dog blew in with the storm but he's not like other dogs write three paragraphs about how Tornado is not like other dogs well Sparky likes people and he's a regular dog what can Tornado do that Sparky couldn't card tricks he does card tricks with Pete soon Molly's Christmas cranberry bread I'll smear with her lemon butter and one morning Bill will phone Joe it's Bill I'll be over in an hour with Beverly's Christmas bread and cookies market quiet this hour of the morning roast for dinner with my mother on Sunday oh Sunday Joe that's sounds good the girls have a special day off from school no Ma it's Sunday oh yes it's Sunday what am I thinking I'll call you Sunday morning which Sunday is that now chicken coffee Irish oatmeal spinach broccoli onions garlic milk butter paper towels soda juice tangerines potatoes dish soap bread ice cream a hundred and ten bucks they rebuilt a city street in Iraq that the surge is working we'll talk to friends of the man who shot ten people in a mall before turning the gun on himself my all-time favorite holiday television commercial when I was a boy the Norelco electric razor little Santa driving the electric razor like a sled across the snow no instead it's asses tits how to stay young and retire with a lot of money need I point out the flaws that man creates in the murky water the clock ticks both hands on one number a year instantly passes the hands move and split a familiar face standing behind the door Celeste reads to me as I write then writes about what she read for her weekend homework smell coffee Irish oatmeal simmering hair dryer upstairs Molly readying for work girls still

sleeping drive to Home Depot pick out a Christmas
tree tie it to the roof Molly and I carry it in house
she strings the lights then the girls wrap the garland
and hang the decorations baked breaded chicken
penne and broccoli Ange writes that she sat next to
Lou Reed Lou Reed writes that he sat next to a mys-
terious poet what numskull would put cheese on
linguine with clams these Americans they ruin
everything they're not American they're Greek oh
what's the difference don't relax don't give in don't
within confines rush or remain at rest I refuse to
restrain my appetite so keeping forever is hard in the
time of no time winter storm warnings tonight real
or artificial trees which are more eco-friendly final
edits on the waiter book finish final student poems
I'm fond of the word nonetheless nonetheless I'm
fond of many words like fond a great golfer in
ancient times when he stepped up to the tee beasts
crouched on the ground birds flew down without
waiting for him to swing his club this was known as
learning not to blink when you swing the club same
thing with the cab driver who could take you any-
where in the blink of an eye who learned by not
blinking for ten years girls upstairs laughing chasing
each other heat blows through the grate my sister
Betty phones my mother should be here around two
they'll come back for her at six roast beef noodles
and salad dish of sorbet time to straighten the living

room shower fold load of laundry now girls argue over whether to leave the quilt on the sofa Celeste comes down crying no one ever takes her ideas seriously the family in the house behind us has never had another yard party since the cops came all those months ago thick ice layer over the windshield sidewalks and streets slick kids slip and fall elderly woman down hard on her back the intersection of Central and Medford pull the car over go to her aid I'm okay she says but she's shaken takes my arm help her up we shuffle our way to the bus stop just hold the pole until the bus comes and the guy riding a bicycle goes down hard gets up and falls again while walking the bike Amanda writes that she could use a drink the house has a lost sippy-cup smell her mother cried the house was filled with balloons everything is fine dear don't worry then Sam cried mop the floor strip the beds take out the garbage walk Sparky find my lost glove right next to the plastic bag filled with Sparky's poop I dropped yesterday morning sweep until there's nothing left if things were equal nothing that snaps would snap

quale [kwa-lay]: *Eng.* n 1. A property (such as hardness) considered apart from things that have that property. 2. A property that is experienced as distinct from any source it may have in a physical object. *Ital.* pron. a. 1. Which, what. 2. Who. 3. Some. 4. As, just as.